HI-TECH HI-TOUCH BRANDING

Creating Brand Power in the

Age of Technology

Paul Temporal
and
K. C. Lee

John Wiley & Sons (Asia) Pte Ltd
Singapore   New York   Chichester
Brisbane   Toronto   Weinheim

S 658. 827 TEM

This publication is designed to provide accurate and authoritative information in regard to the
subject matter covered. It is sold with the understanding that the publisher is not engaged in
rendering professional services. If professional advice or other expert assistance is required, the
services of a competent professional person should be sought.

Other Wiley Editorial Offices

John Wiley & Sons, Inc., 605 Third Avenue, New York, NY 10158-0012, USA
John Wiley & Sons Ltd, Baffins Lane, Chichester, West Sussex PO19 1UD, England
John Wiley & Sons (Canada) Ltd, 22 Worcester Road, Rexdale, Ontario M9W 1L1, Canada
John Wiley & Sons Australia Ltd, 33 Park Road (PO Box 1226), Milton, Queensland 4064,
Australia
Wiley-VCH, Pappelallee 3, 69469 Weinheim, Germany

Library of Congress Cataloging-in-Publication Data
Temporal, Paul.
    Hi-tech hi-touch branding: creating brand power in the age of technology / Paul
Temporal, with K. C. Lee
        p. cm.
    ISBN 0-471-84596-5 (cloth: alk. paper)
        1. Brand name products – Marketing. 2. Electronic commerce. I. Lee, K. C.

HF5415.13 .T395 2000
658-8'27–dc21   00-045590

Typeset in 11/15 points, Goudy by Linographic Services Pte Ltd
Printed in Singapore by Saik Wah Press Pte Ltd
10 9 8 7 6 5 4 3 2 1

Contents

Acknowledgments

We would like to give very special thanks to three people who have helped considerably in the writing of this book, and who have done so in addition to all their other heavy commitments at NCS. They are Eunice Chew Kim Ee, Judy Wong Lee Yoon, and Yew Ker Ling. Without their efforts and ideas, this book would be much less impressive.

Also, the following people are among the many who deserve special mention:

Aaron Boey, Chris Beaumont, Daniel Binns, Sabrina Chin, Kenneth Crolius, Rod Davies, David Haigh, Tim Heberden, Barry Hepburn, Lisa Nocella, Al Ries, Martin Trott, and Ed Zander.

We would also like to thank the following organizations for being most helpful in providing information:

Agilent Technologies, Brand Finance, Hewlett-Packard, Lycos Asia, McCann-Erickson, Philips Consumer Electronics, National Computer Systems, Orient Pacific Century, Shanghai General Motors, and Singapore Telecom.

Finally, we would like to thank the team at John Wiley, especially Nick Wallwork, Janis Soo, Tess Bacalla, and Adeline Lim, for their ongoing support and editorial expertise.

Preface

Brands sell. Brands endure. Brands are valuable. Brands are strategic assets. Brand building as companies know it today has long been acknowledged as the key to wealth creation, while the proliferation of consumer goods in the last two decades has led to the development of branding as the essential, definitive tool for competitive differentiation.

Technology has never really played a great role in the success of commercial enterprise branding until very recently, but now the proliferation of products and services is derived from technology itself. The hi-tech nature of business life today is causing a real strategic problem for companies and their products, because technology is so freely available and product parity so easily achievable. In today's emerging competition, size no longer matters and location is not the mantra of retailing. Standing out from the crowd is an even bigger challenge than before, as more and more players crowd onto a more level playing field.

The explosion of the Internet and e-commerce has also had its impact on consumers, shifting their focus from traditional physical purchasing to cyber buying. The rush is on to catch the wave before it is too late.

As the new commercial revolution takes place, companies used to the old ways of marketing have to learn new technologies, and technology companies have to understand how to market themselves better. The key to standing out from the crowd is still the development of a powerful brand image, but the nature of branding has itself been forced to change. What is emerging from this metamorphosis is a new kind of brand experience for the consumer, offering hi-tech and hi-touch brand interaction.

This book looks at branding in the digital age—what applies from the past, and what new rules are unfolding that will create the success stories of tomorrow.

The essence of the book

This book is a review of branding in the twenty-first century. It looks at what has changed and what has not, which rules still apply and which are now redundant, what works and what does not, and how branding is different for technology companies, products, and services. It is not the end of the story by any means, even if the new rules of branding are presented here. Changes to these rules may still happen in the near future. However, we are confident that what has been written will serve as our guide as we venture further down the path of technological change, at least for the foreseeable future.

Hi-tech branding can be interpreted to mean two things. It can mean how companies are using technology to assist their brand-building efforts, or how the companies dealing in hi-tech products and services are, or should be, employing branding techniques. The book covers both, and you will find plenty of examples from many industries.

Who should read this book?

The obvious answer is anyone that is involved in branding. But the implications of what is being said here make this book imperative reading for:
- chief executives who are dealing with change and new technologies
- entrepreneurs and those new hi-tech businesses
- company executives involved in electronic commerce
- technology managers and all others involved in new product development
- managers for strategic planning
- marketing and sales directors and managers
- brand and category managers

- advertising, promotion, research, and media agencies
- business educators and students of management and marketing

Foreword

The present millennium hails a new era, with new customer expectations and new competitive realities. Technological innovation and the increasing speed of innovation itself necessitate that all companies regularly reflect on and reinvent their way to market. In this *Brand New World*, it is far better to own the heart and mind of the consumer than it is the factory—what the product/service does is less important than what the brand stands for. Moving ahead, the brand will become more important.

Brands, and the brand owners, will succeed because when there is increasing choice, and these are new choices, increasing complexity, and less time, the consumer will rely on strong brands more than ever, because they will do better what they have always done: simplify choice. As people's lives become more fragmented and, yet paradoxically, they become better connected and informed—brand management will need to rely less on traditional mass marketing vehicles to create a mosaic of coherent brand experiences, where the messaging content reflects the different context in which brands contact their target customer. Managing a brand's character will be a strategic imperative, with major brand opportunities created from multiple vantage points/disciplines—not only advertising, but also experiential branding, corporate identity, CRM, promotions, reputation management, and everything else that influences consumer thinking and experience.

This is a timely text by Paul Temporal and K.C. Lee, who clearly and pragmatically articulate from a holistic perspective the primacy of brands and branding for any "new economy" company. They rightly view technology as an enabler in brand management and not necessarily a sustainable point of difference, even for technology based companies.

Chris D. Beaumont
EVP, Chief Strategy Officer Asia-Pacific
McCann-Erickson WorldGroup

1

The Technology Century

The world of technology is changing very fast, and is changing the world as a result. For instance, the latest amazing breakthrough concerning the draft mapping of the human gene system—the genome project—carried out jointly by thousands of scientists worldwide, would never have been possible without advances in technology. It will change the world in many fundamental ways, some too early to predict now.

Other examples of technology advancement abound, and this chapter summarizes where the world is in many areas of technological change. But one inescapable fact is that, increasingly, companies in this hi-tech world have to rely on branding to differentiate themselves in these cluttered and fast-moving markets.

TECHNOLOGY CONVERGENCE

Si Ying, who is in primary 4, asked her mother about her English homework, which was due the next day. Her teacher wanted her to define the word *margay*. But neither her mother nor her father knew what the word meant, so they asked her to look it up in the dictionary. The young girl countered that the word was not in any of the six dictionaries they had at home. Noting that the library was already closed by this time, the couple decided to call a friend who was known to have a good command of English. Unfortunately, he did not know the word's meaning either.

"Maybe the school wants your child to be creative in defining a new word, as the Ministry of Education!Ns pushing the concept of 'Thinking School, Thinking Nation' hard," the friend said jokingly. Perhaps the word means "martian gay," he added, throwing everyone into a fit of laughter.

Still groping for a definition of the word, Si Ying hit upon an idea: "Why don't we try the Internet?" Si Ying's mother was bowled over by her daughter's suggestion. An information technology (IT) professional, she wondered why she hadn't thought of this solution first. Immediately, they logged on to the Internet, selected a search engine, and keyed in the word *margay*. It didn't take long before they finally learned its meaning—a spotted American cat!

In recent years a remarkable infusion of technologies into homes, schools, and businesses has changed and expanded learning opportunities for children. It has brought about new possibilities for continued lifelong learning. Much of this revolution in learning technologies can be attributed to the development of the personal computer (PC), which altered our beliefs about technology, our access to it, and its role in our lives. Technology has advanced so fast that it has not only changed the rules of competition in the business world, it also has had a great impact on the way we work, acquire knowledge, purchase our groceries, and communicate with others. Technology today is so pervasive it affects everything we do and everyone in almost every field of endeavor, whether we like it or not.

As the scope of technology is wide, we will focus our discussion on telecommunications and computing technology. Telecommunications may seem to have changed the least. For most users, telecommunications is still characterized by the phone on the wall, the desk, or the waist belt, seemingly providing an analog, low-fidelity communications channel for voice communications. Behind the scenes, however, there has been a technical revolution in both the transmission and switching technology used. To a large extent, this revolution has remained invisible to the user.

Probably the most visible technological revolution in the last 30 years has been seen in computing. Computers have moved from being exotic and rare mainframes to disposable commodities on every desk—

be it at home or at work. Stand-alone personal computers are increasingly connected to some form of network that allows people to access information stored on central file servers or to communicate with other PCs. As a result, they are rapidly becoming the key interface between humans and electronic media. This is obviously true in business, and is fast becoming so in the home. The home information/ entertainment terminal will increasingly combine the functionality of the television, telephone, PC, radio, CD player, and video camera. Already, the clearest evidence of convergence is happening in the business and telecommuting communities, which increasingly exploit both computing and communications.

The availability of low-cost, high-resolution displays has also made possible the development and operation of the more advanced man-machine interface (MMI) such as graphical user interface (GUI), "touch screen," multi-media, and "browser." These new MMIs take advantage of three of our most powerful sensory systems, namely, sight, hearing, and touch. (Who knows, the computer of the future may emit a fragrance and raise your appetite to cover the other two human sensory systems!) One clear advantage that the electronic medium already has over its printed counterparts is its ability to operate interactively. Certainly the future lies with "voice recognition" through which a computer can translate the voice into digital commands to perform computing functions, thus eliminating the need for typing.

Driving all these fundamental changes are the costs and related benefits of basic components and the design technologies on which they are based. The two technologies of electronics and photonics have so shifted the balance of advantage that all electronic systems are being driven to use digital techniques. Hence, we find major sectors of the electronics industry using similar technology, leading to strong synergies between communications, computing, cable, broadcasting, and consumer electronics, and blurring the technical distinctions between these industrial sectors in the process.

The last 20 years have also seen the growing dominance of computer software-defined systems as opposed to hardware-defined systems. In the latter, we envisage a circuit that has been designed and wired to carry out a certain function, and nothing more. In the realm of computers, we recognize the power that software has given us to switch from word processor to spreadsheet to database to HTML at the click of a mouse. The complexity of some of these programs and the increasing need to integrate and implement these systems have given rise to a wide variety of services. The IT services market has in the past five years been growing at a compound annual growth rate (CAGR) of at least 25% to 30% worldwide, according to Gartner Group. International companies such as EDS U.S., CSC U.S., Gap Gemini of Germany, and NCS of Singapore have become key partners to hardware and software big names such as IBM, Hewlett-Packard, Compaq, Sun Microsystems, and Microsoft.

The liberalization of the telecommunications industry

In 1999 the liberalization of telecommunications services provided for in the World Trade Organization agreement came into effect, leading to a huge expansion of those services. The agreement covered a full range of data and voice services, including fixed lines, satellite, and cellular systems. As a result, the world communications market is expected to grow to US$1,000 billion by 2001 from US$70 billion in 1999.

The principal force behind the rapid changes in telecommunications has been the move toward digital technology and away from analog formats. The most stunning technical changes, which have appeared only in the past four years, have come as engineers began to discover that they could pack far more information into any communications line with a variety of digital signal-compression techniques and wider bandwidth. These techniques can expand the capacity of wireless or wireline systems tenfold, or even more, at a lower cost.

As a result, there has been a fundamental shift in the displacement of voice traffic by data traffic. In fact, it is estimated that within the next few years (estimates vary by year), over 80% of global communications traffic will contain data, leading to an enormous shortage of bandwidth. This growth is largely due to the Internet.

The development of enormous low-cost transmission and storage capacity promises to change the very nature of the telecommunications sector and its services. For example, viewers will be able to order a program from a remote "server" (computer) that can deliver a movie or other stored video product of their choice to their households at any time. Any viewer will be able to stop, rewind, fast-forward, or otherwise control the delivery of this product. Each viewer may be able to interact with other viewers, say, in the playing of video games. Eventually, subscribers may have a wide variety of interactive broadband services, although no one knows what these services will be.

These technological forces are propelling all communications media toward a single, ubiquitous digital network that is in general called an "information superhighway." Many assume that the myriad of companies in the local telephone, long-distance telephone, and cable television industries are about to coalesce into one large, interactive, terrestrial network with a variety of interconnected wireless adjuncts.

The "net" result of this tremendous transformation is that consumers today have access, and will have more in the future, to unparalleled amounts of information and new technologies. The twenty-first century will indeed come to be known as the age of technology or the technology century. Technology is undoubtedly changing people's lives and the rules of competition in business, and totally reshaping markets.

The Internet era

Nowhere is technological change more evident than in the Internet. The result of a research program by the U.S. Department of Defense as protection for military installations against nuclear attacks during the late 1960s, the Internet gained popularity when research agencies and universities flocked to join the network a decade later. By the mid-1990s the Internet had gained general public awareness; it now dominates individual and corporate communications thinking. It is a massive network of computers that are linked together forming what is commonly known as the information superhighway.

The World Wide Web (the Web, or WWW)—the graphical interface of the Internet—was created in 1989 at the European Laboratory for Particle Physics through the introduction of "hypertext" links, which gave us access to vast amounts of information. The Internet and the Web are now part of everyday conversations across most of the world, and influence billions of dollars of IT investment each year.

The Internet's profile was greatly enhanced in 1998 as company start-ups embarked on equity raising in the United States. By then the Internet was no longer seen as a gee-whiz product but as a real business with real revenue-generating ability, be it through access subscriptions, advertising, or e-commerce. It is remarkable how quickly the Internet was adopted as a business application. Internet adoption was three times faster than that for TV, and ten times faster than for radio. The Internet has had a meteoric rise fuelled by its ability to change the way people interact with each other—from e-mail to shopping to politics to culture. Consider this: radio needed 38 years to attract 50 million listeners, while TV needed 13 years to draw 50 million viewers. But the Internet took only four years to gain 50 million users. Indeed, the Internet has changed the way we live.

Yet the story is still unfolding, as more and more people discover the value of the Internet and the different ways in which it can be used, and as a growing number of innovations associated with it are released. The Internet we know today is like a baby who will eventually grow up into an adult that will be very hard to recognize.

The real impact of the Internet has so far been in the area of business-to-business marketing relationships, because it offers organizations the chance to do all or part of their business online. It is here that the real gains in the short to medium term will be achieved. In fact, some say that this use of the Internet will always be dominant. Yet there is no doubt that in the long term, business-to-consumer marketing will likewise continue to accelerate on the Internet as more families get connected. From sports to savings and loans, from music to medicine, from news to nutrition, from education to the environment, from fashion to fun, there is something on the Internet for everyone.

As a result, the speed with which people are taking to the Internet is astonishing. There are currently 220 million people on the Net, and the number is rising fast. In a 1999 survey commissioned by America Online (AOL) to the Roper organization for people with access to the Internet, the respondents were asked what one form of media they would choose to take if they were to be stranded on a desert island. Sixty-eight percent said the Internet, 28% the telephone, and 8% TV.

In both business-to-business and business-to-consumer cases, however, the Internet will bring about major, irreversible changes in the way global and local businesses operate. The importance attached to technology in business is underscored by a 1999 estimate by *The Economist* that 42% of capital investment in the United States is spent on enhancing information technology. What is also important to note is that the technological innovations that have taken place in the Internet revolution are in fact only enablers, meaning they enable businesses to develop customer relationships. The section on customer relationship management in Chapter 5 discusses this subject further.

Net effects

Since ancient times, new technologies have increased the durability and portability of information. The distribution of information also influences its credibility, its spread, and its impact on social behavior (learning from others exposes one to new values and culture, and vice versa). Moreover, the distribution of relationships affects future information exchange (you talk to whomever you know), which usually benefits the parties involved in many ways (e.g., education, collaboration, innovation). Technologies have not caused complete social upheavals—the change is more subtle and long-lasting. This fact can be examined by studying the level of benefit that each group derives from interaction; some positive and negative consequences are derived from exchange—the net effect on each group depends on the balance of consequences.

The Internet has fundamentally changed our lives by:

- facilitating access to information and commerce by anyone anytime, anywhere, and anyhow

- integrating work, home, and leisure
- providing for the purchase of digital goods and services anywhere, anytime
- blurring the physical barriers, boundaries, and time zones between producers and consumers, who are now actively involved in the actual product design process such as when they enter a virtual car showroom and configure an automobile on the computer screen from a massive variety of design choices
- changing the rules of competition—for example, with e-newspapers. (Who could have thought that the Encyclopaedia Britannica would be offered free?)
- deconstructing the traditional business value chain, in some cases taking out intermediaries, such as distributors, in the marketing process
- creating whole new market segments, such as the e-citizen and Generation-N, and their sub-segments
- creating knowledge-based businesses, such as Yahoo. These businesses quickly adjust their offerings to changing circumstances, customize them, and enable customers to use them in real time.

As we explore the nature of information, it is just as important to study the people using it as it is to study the technology itself. The types of benefits derived from technology ultimately depend on the environment of the users exposed to it. The Internet newsgroups, for example, are a wonderful reminder that the effects of technology are unpredictable and often surprising. This emerging "network community" seems to be a truly interesting phenomenon that changes both people's relationships and the nature of information.

Amid all these dazzling changes are many new opportunities and challenges. But "getting it" requires a change of mindset, and making things happen in this brave new world needs a new way of thinking about strategic marketing. Branding has not escaped the proverbial sword, with new rules still being written. It is an exciting stage of development to be in, but not one for the faint-hearted.

Electronic commerce

The whole world is buzzing with talk of e-commerce, one of the major outcomes of the Internet revolution. Even U.S. President Bill Clinton, who openly admits he is "technologically challenged," has made e-purchases "all by himself," according to an aide. What is happening in this online business explosion, and how can companies use branding to help their e-commerce business?

In the digital economy, size and location are no longer as relevant to business opportunities as they used to be. The underlying notion of such an economy is immediacy—where product life cycles are shortening dramatically and time to market is shrinking. Companies that are able to leverage real-time business processes and are alert to market needs will become the leaders in the race. The ones who will be left behind are companies that are not exploiting the power of the Internet to gain market share, reduce transaction costs, and shorten the time to market. Incumbent companies may lose market leadership to e-commerce companies if they do not re-think their business strategy and deploy Internet commerce.

In the digital era, it is not enough for an established company to have a network of strategically located stores to cater to its wide customer base. This tack could have diminishing effects when a new company establishes a global chain using Internet commerce within a much shorter time frame. What used to be a strategic competitive advantage for the incumbent could become a disadvantage, because the new company can sell its products at a lower price and achieve a higher margin.

In addition to enabling global reach, Internet commerce shortens the intermediary value chain. With Internet commerce, the new player can shorten its time to market because it need not deal with the middlemen. Company managers and directors urgently need to look seriously at how the Internet concept is changing the business world. The Internet was initially thought of as a passing fad, and companies did not grasp the benefits of e-commerce. However, as existing businesses may crumble before an onslaught of new Internet commerce companies, more and more organizations are embarking on leveraging the power of the Internet.

This relentless rise of e-commerce poses certain questions to established businesses, namely:

- Is our business suited to it?
- How should we go about it?
- How should it fit with our existing channels?
- How can we use it to strengthen the brand?
- How best do we represent our brand on the Net?

Before we answer these questions, we should look at why e-commerce is so compelling for companies wishing to create brand power. The reason lies in one simple concept—mass customization. The Internet gives companies the ability to tailor every transaction to each customer, and save money at the same time!

MASS CUSTOMIZATION

The pressure exerted by certain types of customers insisting that they be treated differently has pushed the global trend of market fragmentation. These audiences have enough critical mass to make companies pay attention to them. As a result, generic global products have developed with enough flexibility to cater to customized differences. Fashion and luxury goods are typical outputs of this shift. However, with the introduction of the Internet, customization has moved to a new level.

Consider the virtual changing room. Gucci, Debenhams, and Marks & Spencer are putting together a joint venture with an Internet company that will let customers "try on" clothes and sample make-up on screen. Shoppers will be able to create 3D models of themselves and scan in details of their facial features. They will also be able to tell how the clothes look on them from all angles, and can use any standard Web browser to do so. Even the big brand names are catering to rising consumer expectations and differentiating themselves from other brands available on the Net. All this shows that e-commerce is now becoming a crowded market, just like the high street, while differentiation has become essential.

DISINTERMEDIATION

There has been much talk in marketing circles of late about how the Internet has eroded the classic value chain of business. This phenomenon is commonly referred to as *disintermediation*, which term is sometimes used wrongly.

Disintermediation refers to a situation where at least one section of the distribution chain is removed. A good example of this is Dell Computer (www.dell.com), a company that allows consumers to configure their own computers and then order direct from the manufacturer who delivers straight to them. The computer distributor or agent is the casualty.

An example of where non-disintermediation takes place is the online trading of securities/investments by Charles Schwab, which replaces only the direct sale from person to person. Similarly, Amazon.com is selling direct online but is not reducing the number of distribution levels. Rather, it is merely replacing the traditional physical bookstore intermediary. Convenient and cheaper it may be, but it is the replacement of one channel by another.

It is not just the Internet that is driving these changes in distribution, but technology in general. Telephone banking, for example, is not Internet banking but a channel replacement driven by technology.

Toward customer convenience

Hi-tech products and services are theoretically meant to make daily life easier for consumers, and some companies work hard on achieving this objective.

Take the example of Southwest Airlines. This company appears to be beating its rivals on Net buying. According to the Nielsen/Net Ratings' August 1999 survey, 13.85% of people who visited the airline's site bought a ticket. The booking ratio is evidently twice that of other travel firms on the Net, such as Travelocity. Part of the answer seems to lie in providing the consumer with a page that needs only ten clicks to complete the transaction. The key focus is service, and a fast one at that. Microsoft's brand promise appears to be not just compatibility but ease. We just wish these companies would get rid of more bugs before they pushed new releases. Failure to deliver on the brand promise will harm their brand image.

E-COMMERCE IS NOT FOR EVERYONE

The costs of developing an e-commerce business strategy can be high; for some companies they are too high. It was precisely for this reason that Levi Strauss & Co. has decided to stop selling jeans and other products online after less than a year of doing business via the Web. Instead, it has decided to bring retailers online to sell its products, including JC Penney Co. and the Macy's chain. The sites www.levi.com and www.dockers.com will be maintained for marketing purposes, and will be used to advertise products and direct customers to where they can buy the company's products. As has been pointed out, the company made this decision not because online sales were poor—sales were in fact strong—but, as spokesman Jeff Beckman said, the numbers just did not stack up, given "how expensive it is to run a world-class commercial site." Maintaining good relationships with retailers was also part of the decision, as they were not allowed to sell the company's products online when Levi Strauss itself was doing so.

Manufacturers then have to consider how e-commerce will affect their relationships with existing distributors and retailers, in addition to its impact on the cost elements. Of course, if you are in control of your brand through distribution and sales channels, the problem is removed.

Retailers also have to factor in certain considerations if they are going to supplement their traditional selling activities with online services. For example, they will have to integrate their current computer systems for handling orders, and managing inventory and transactions, with their Net business. They will also have to make allowances for customer service, which needs to be active 24 hours a day, seven days a week, and spread out the marketing effort between physical and virtual stores.

Impact of convergence on business

We are witnessing a great convergence, as computers join with global telecommunications to build a new trading or business platform—one with extraordinary speed and scope. This new market, however, is disembodied: it exists nowhere and everywhere. The information superhighway is global, so where you live and work matters less than how you are connected. Successful businesses in the new environment will use its tools creatively. The convergence of communications and computers has the potential to enrich communication and analysis throughout any set of business activities. Convergence is, as a result, one of the broadest and most powerful enablers of business change today.

Technology evolution is altering the definition of work, the process of working, and the required competence of knowledge workers. Hence, we no longer think of FedEx as a big deal. Even faxing has become cumbersome with the advent of voice mail and e-mail. Of course, there is almost no time or patience left for paper-based correspondence, or "snail mail," as it is called today. When we want to reach someone, we e-mail, page, or call him on the mobile phone, and we get upset if the person does not respond immediately. With technology at our fingertips, we are expected to do things *now*, which means 24 hours a day, seven days a week!

Progressive companies are making the day-to-day work routine more flexible, thus moving away from the nine-to-five cycle. With the advent of the laptop, work and play easily mix. Turning on a home computer late at night to check e-mail messages is extremely common nowadays.

Many of us have probably heard the Wal-Mart story—how it was successfully transformed from a relatively small company in a rural area of the United States to an international brand by creating a complete business system. Wal-Mart developed, and continues to refine, an offer that customers find nearly irresistible: low prices on a variety of brands. In recent years, Wal-Mart began to experiment with convergence technologies by:

- understanding and responding to customers' changing desires using computers to analyze vast quantities of customer transaction data and sniff out consumer buying patterns
- setting up an efficient distribution system that would serve as the hub of joint purchasing, shared facilities, systematic ordering, and store-level distribution of a large number of goods
- managing communications and control of a network of remotely located stores, which required close monitoring of a carefully drawn set of measures transmitted daily to Wal-Mart headquarters
- building a set of incentives and measures that would ensure the commitment of employees and managers to local stores. This effort led to a complex system of training, management, bonus, and stock-purchase plans for employees

Today, with the continued improvement of these systems, Wal-Mart's checkout scanners feed inventory data via satellite back to the company's regional distribution centers where products are sent down high-speed conveyers to trucks responsible for daily inventory deliveries to individual stores. The company's databases facilitate the achievement of true economies of scale in terms of product inventories at each store. With convergence technologies, Wal-Mart can share detailed information on what is selling at individual locations and collectively tailor inventories to the needs of each customer. As a result, the company should be able to keep up with emerging consumer trends and evolve accordingly over the years.

For Wal-Mart, convergence has provided tools for the creation of a service platform, where the cost of serving each additional customer—and of knowing each customer personally—continues to decline with the scale of the total customer body served. The only thing that keeps the Wal-Mart growth in check is that over the past few years Kmart, Sears, and others have finally replicated the price/performance system of the whole Wal-Mart business system. However, the competition will not so much be on the convergent technology used, as on the efficiency and scale of the whole business system.

The Wal-Mart case is just one of a class of new, convergence-enabled global business designs. These business architectures focus on creating broad orchestration of the contributions of many players. In the case of Wal-Mart, orchestration consists of disciplining suppliers and shaping the behavior of its network of stores. The Wal-Mart brand, so famous in the United States, is now marching through Europe en route to becoming a global brand with the help of technology.

Whether you are a customer or a producer, the pace of innovation is so swift that shorter and shorter product cycles place even greater pressure on the one thing that is bound to stay—the brand. Businesses no longer compete only with those that are physically present in your market. Any Web-based business from any part of the world could be your competitor. So every day your customers have tens, if not hundreds, of new competitors to choose from. How do you win? By establishing a relationship that transcends the neighborhood—more to the point, by building a powerful brand with all the emotional associations that go with it.

Impact of convergence on the home

What is the state of technology in the home? What are the social forces that have contributed to the evolution of the household as a media environment?

In most U.S., European, and Asian households, the TV programming schedule generally anchors the range of potential evening activities and sets the limits of information consumption. With cable TV, a typical 30-channel system makes available 240 half-hour programs in four hours. However, most programs arrive in a totally fragmented way, with the content of one showing no apparent connection to the next. If the watcher has a lingering interest in a subject, there is no way to continue once the program ends. But all of this is changing. For example, in Singapore, with the SingaporeONE ("One Network for Everyone") infrastructure and SingTel Magix service, users can now select the program they would like to watch anytime, anywhere.

It is interesting to note that the number of persons per household has fallen consistently throughout the twentieth century. The number of single-person households has also risen. Both of these developments have occurred at a time when Americans have increased the number of computing devices in their homes.

One growing fragment deserves note. Millions of people are now working at home because the time-honored tradition of self-employment has combined with a push by corporations to hold down costs by outsourcing work. The result is that some Americans have converted their homes into centers of production, while others split work time between home and office. Such use of the home and of media is possible due to the remarkable convergence of information technologies today.

With the arrival of new interactive technologies, some households will use television like computers, while others will use computers like TV sets. The home has always been a social environment first and foremost; therefore, if one wishes to understand it, one must grapple with its social themes. The themes that once defined the old boundaries—between work and home, between public and private life, between labor and leisure—no longer appear so clear. The lack of clarity stems, in part, from a century-long pattern of increased information consumption, during which people combined work and home life, public and private life, labor and leisure by building a media environment in the home. In so doing, they have evolved new media uses for negotiating simultaneous messages through multiple channels, thanks to the convergence of information technologies.

In terms of buying decisions at home, as families browse together, children, who are probably more Web-savvy than their parents, wield a lot of influence. (We may put the Net generation here, as branding must consider this.)

Impact on education and the learning organization concept

Researchers at Stanford Research Institute and Educational Development Corporation found that hypermedia tends to encourage learners to actively process complex tasks within a collaborative context while employing higher-order thinking skills. So while the study found that technology increases teacher workload, teachers were willing to use technology because learners were more motivated and seemed to learn more.

Aside from homes and educational institutions, technology can also have an enormous impact on learning organizations. In his book *The Fifth Discipline*, Peter Senge describes a learning organization as one in which "people are continually learning how to learn together." Since learning is a social process of interaction, a primary function of technology should be to facilitate interaction between the functional units of a firm, thereby encouraging a learning environment. Learning on the institutional level can be defined as "the systemic capacity to change the codified models an organization uses to interpret and act upon information," said Senge. Such a capacity can be provided by technology to create a synergistic institutional intelligence, or one in which the effectiveness of the organization is greater than the sum of its employees' individual talents.

In an effort to capitalize on the technology–people interface, some companies go all out to produce a "wired workforce." Delta Airlines, for example, offers computers and Internet access to 72,000 staff by joining up with PeoplePC. Delta said this move would afford every employee "the ability to connect to the company electronically." Ford Motor Company, on the other hand, gives its 350,000 staff free computers and printers, as well as Internet access for a small charge. By doing so it aims to keep its employees "at the leading edge of e-business technology and skills" and "unleash the power of the Internet" on its global workforce. According to Ford chief executive Jac Nasser, the company is "committed to serving consumers better by understanding how they think and act. Having a computer and Internet access in the home will accelerate the development of these skills, provide information across our business, and offer opportunities to streamline our processes."

The faster pace of events that occur in modern commerce demands faster systems of processing information, much like the automated displays that guide fighter pilots. These systems perform four functions (the faster they are, the more effective they become): sensing environment signals, interpreting the meaning of the signals captured, determining the appropriate response from a list of options, and executing the response selected. If the results of the action are monitored and interpreted to modify actions in the future, a learning loop is established and an adaptive system is created, which can observe the chaotic signals of the environment and teach itself to act accordingly.

Technology can augment each of the above four tasks for its users, assuming it does not perform the entire loop by itself. Examples of systems that assist in this process are data models (which identify relevant patterns in raw data), neural networks (which analyze data and create new models for optimum interpretation of data), and enterprise models (which link previously fragmented parts of the learning loop into an integrated system). These tools will give rise to the use of virtual reality to control computerized representations of otherwise tangible assets. The task at hand for modern managers will be organizing and deploying information and knowledge, not merely capital, labor, or equipment. All of this will be possible in the twenty-first century only if a firm has the necessary resources to implement such a system, if it can develop an accurate business model, and if it can differentiate between bad models and bad decisions.

Technology affords learners the opportunity to become more active participants in their own learning, and encourages collaboration within and outside the classroom. Younger generations are used to doing several things at once.

It also seems clear that technology can be an important catalyst for educational restructuring and reform—from local to national and international levels. In many advanced countries, students in other schools can attend courses and lessons conducted in the top schools by accessing their syllabi and course materials through the Internet.

Technology industries

Industries such as the computer or telecommunications businesses are facing an intense environmental turbulence due to the increased mobility of information and global workforce. Knowledge and expertise can be transported instantaneously around the world, and any advantage gained by one company can be eliminated by competitive improvements overnight. To stay in the race, a company must be adept at employing a process of innovation—combining market and technology know-how, and mixing this with the creative talents of knowledge workers to solve a constant stream of complex problems. It will also need the ability to derive value from information.

Its key competency will be continuous generation and dissemination of knowledge, stitched together from information and expertise. Companies must ensure that processes are in place for identifying unique problems and opportunities, solving problems, and developing teams.

Technology-based industries have four unique characteristics:

a) high growth

b) rapid change

c) fragmentation (the top IT firms capture less than 20% of the market share)

d) relatively lower marketing and branding expenses, especially for technology service companies.

In the new century, however, technology vendors cannot just rely on technological merits to win in this fragmented industry. They will have to adopt a mass customization approach, and deliver the right message to the right buyer, be it the CEO of a large corporation or the owner of a small company. Branding will become more important, as parity increases and relationships become more necessary.

In recent years, some technology vendors have mirrored the successful branding efforts of other industries. "Cisco Systems, 3Com, Bay Networks, and Cabletron Systems have begun to realize that a brand identity can bring significant advantages in achieving business growth," said Sandy Cals-Summers, industry analyst for Dataquest's Networking

Europe program. "Branding can result in a customer franchise effect, whereby customers demand certain brands and refuse substitutes."

By implementing branding strategies, technology vendors stand to gain that crucial identity, as well as provide users with a value proposition. With a strong brand in place, successful vendors can expect to gain an extra, powerful source of competitive advantage. For instance, historically, one would think of Intel as anything but a marketing-driven organization. Today, however, Intel's brand recognition is among the highest in all sectors of industry. What makes this achievement even more impressive is that Intel sells little directly to end users.

What is the driving force behind Intel's transformation? Intense competitive paranoia. Because Intel must protect its staggering share of the market, the company must not only react to market changes but also invoke changes. But more importantly, Intel has had to develop trust in the marketplace, which it has done through skillfully applied branding techniques. Chapter 3 explains why technology companies should brand their companies, products, and services.

The knowledge economy

The convergence of information technologies and the emergence of high-bandwidth networks will likely have a greater impact on the nature of work than did the telephone at the turn of the last century. The reason behind this dramatic transformation is not the exciting, digital, networked multimedia technology, but the coming of technology convergence and high-bandwidth networks at a moment in history where work itself is being redefined. An obsolescent industrial age is giving way to a knowledge era where significant value-added is found in the continuous creation and communication of new perspectives.

A world-class knowledge worker spends time developing his capacity to perceive, think creatively, and communicate more effectively. He understands that knowledge is not a commodity to be transferred or consumed like a hamburger, but a perspective and a set of practices created by a particular community and that is continuously evolving in language and action. He is keenly aware that his capacity to learn is the only transferable skill he has, that skillful conversations with trusting colleagues lead to new perspectives, and that language creates the future.

Knowledge is replacing capital and energy as the primary wealth-creating asset, just as the latter two replaced land and labor 200 years ago. In addition, technological developments in the last century have transformed the majority of wealth-creating work from being physically-based to "knowledge-based." How and why this happened is explained by the degree to which the world economy has become information-intensive, and by the unique economic attributes of information and information technology.

Information has many properties that differentiate it from tangible assets—it tends to increase in value as it is shared, and you can give it away without giving it up. Because of these differences, information is rarely managed the way other wealth-creating assets are. Technology can be used to give information more value-in-use by codifying, storing, processing, and presenting it in a way that increases knowledge, provided the information is timely, accurate, and applicable to the task at hand. Mere facts have little value without being narrowed in scope to the particular problem, drawing inferences from the data to discover relationships, and synthesizing those relationships into knowledge that can affect decisions and increase wealth.

IT can change the value of information simply by processing it faster, giving a manager more time to explore available options, or allowing him to decide faster. IT can also allow a business to organize, manage, and link multiple sources of information and their users.

Connecting and sharing information among the different departments of a firm can give each participant a unified sense of "what's going on out there" and "how we are doing things here." The results of using technology to share information and connect users come in the form of increased understanding or intelligence, but these results are only as obtainable as decisions are made from the information. They are reflections of how technology changes information into an active force for wealth creation.

While technologies show significant promise in supporting a radical rethinking of the traditional concepts and processes of branding, the effort must begin with our thinking, not with the seductive technologies.

The future

It is doubtful whether anyone can predict the evolution of technology in the next ten or 20 years any more than he could have predicted in 1974 that the AT&T dynasty would end in 1984. Or that anyone would be able to carry a portable telephone handset weighing only a few ounces and costing only a handful of dollars. Predicting the future is always dangerous. However, a vision of a more technology-rich tomorrow, even if it becomes dated in a few years, may contribute to a realization of the potential that technologies hold. What will never be wrong is that technology is perpetually changing, and that branding will remain vital to the success of any company operating in a crowded market.

2

Introduction to Branding

BRANDING AS A VITAL ASPECT OF CORPORATE STRATEGY

Since the late 1980s, branding has become one of the most talked-about subjects among managers. It figures on the boardroom agendas of nearly all the major companies in the world. Branding has evolved mainly in the fast-moving consumer goods industries, where substantial profits accruing from brands have attracted a great deal of attention. Brands are now treated as strategic assets in their own right by many firms, and brand valuation is a rapidly emerging business.

Slow to catch on to the benefits of branding have been companies that are steeped in technology. Even if they have been producing goods for public, as opposed to business, consumption, they have shown some reticence in embarking on brand investment. Where it is commonplace to spend large amounts of money on plant and capital equipment in technology-based industries, investing in brands has been relatively ignored. As a result, there are few powerful technology brands, and yet they would seem to be in desperate need of branding as a major tool to differentiate themselves from all their competitors.

The world of parity

Perhaps one of the reasons why technology companies have not given branding high priority is that technology product and service markets have not been very cluttered until the last decade of the twentieth century. Whereas by the beginning of the 1990s consumer goods markets had in many cases reached the stage of maturity where they were at bursting point with a proliferation of products, technology has only recently reached this stage.

But now the world of parity has hit technology markets as well. And technology itself has hastened this adverse situation. In the twenty-first century, it is so much easier to copy a competitor's products, services, or systems that the name of the game now is how to stand out from the crowd. Technology is becoming a commodity business, and the relatively established hi-tech companies that find themselves being sucked into the commodity trap, such as Sun Microsystems, are now realizing the role branding plays in staying out of it.

Shorter life cycles

Another factor that has awoken technology companies to the fact that branding is important is the relentless decline of product life cycles, which have been reduced to a matter of weeks from what used to be years. Faced with such frightening product change, and with competitors continuously bringing new products to market and enhancing others, brands are literally the only things that represent stability to both companies and consumers. In fact, there is now a growing realization among technology companies that brands need not have life cycles— they can last indefinitely. This is a massive attraction.

Converging and new technologies

As if product proliferation and life cycle decompression were not enough, technology companies now find themselves surrounded by collapsing market boundaries, driven by the convergence of technologies. Companies can leap industries by simply acquiring the necessary technology, and where companies thought they understood the nature of the competition, they are astonished at how quickly things can change. Ten years ago, companies such as Time Warner would never have imagined merging with Internet-based companies such as AOL. The Internet was just not in the public domain then. But it is the powerful brands that always win the battle for market dominance in this fast-changing world.

Return on investment

Pouring money into technology can be a wrong move unless you have a brand that really stands for something in the minds of consumers. Powerful brands provide both consumer trust and high returns. Consumers will not buy from companies that do not have a good brand image, particularly in technology markets where the products are not fully understood. They will only buy trusted brands. Developing a brand is not cheap, but the returns can be spectacular. Strong brands can command premium prices wherever they choose to go, and can often be worth more than the net asset value of the business enterprise.

Importance of branding to hi-tech companies

The accelerating and turbulent nature of technological change poses problems to those trying to establish, develop, and manage their brands. Technology-based companies are faced with perpetual change, and this seemingly goes against the whole basis of branding, which is consistency. So one of the dilemmas for hi-tech companies is how to balance the two. An additional problem is product parity. In a world where anything physical can be copied with amazing speed, there is little room for the traditional unique selling proposition. Launch a new product on the shelves, and your competitors will have a similar, possibly improved one, in a relatively short span of time. Lastly, the cautious nature of consumer decision making with regard to technology products makes life more difficult for technology-based firms when trying to persuade consumers to buy. In these circumstances, which appear to be intensifying, branding becomes even more important. Good branding will help a company overcome all of these problems, while poor branding will only make things worse.

It is thus time for technology companies to venture into branding in a significant way. With a strong brand comes market power. It is all very well to have a good-quality product or service (in fact, it is essential to survival), but it is your brand that will make your company succeed in very congested markets. It is as well to remember that quality can be copied too, and that while you will never develop a powerful brand without quality, this element alone will never be enough to differentiate your company, product, or service from the competition.

With 50 to 60 software companies starting up each month in Silicon Valley alone, the hi-tech marketplace is becoming like a busy main road during rush hour. Not only does branding matter in the new hi-tech world, it is even more important than in the traditional consumer products markets. For the Internet and software businesses, branding is a prerequisite for market entry. Gone are the days when a company could take its time to develop a brand. Only a strong brand will help hi-tech companies to survive through immediate and lasting differentiation.

Like any sphere of management practice, branding does not stand still. It is a dynamic activity, because it is subject to the forces of change. In this age of technology, some things have remained the same in brand creation, management, and development, while others have inevitably changed. Companies would do well to bear these things in mind.

BRANDING IN THE DIGITAL AGE

Whether your company is a technology enterprise or not, you cannot avoid getting involved in technology—the Digital Age is here, and branding is here to stay. But branding is not new, although admittedly it has only risen to prominence in the last 20 years or so. So it is interesting to ask what has *not* changed in the world of branding, or what principles of branding are still relevant to hi-tech companies. Conversely, it is also interesting to ask what has changed—that is, what new things must be considered in the branding of technology companies and products, and how we should adapt traditional branding to the digital world.

What has not changed in the world of branding?

Several things about branding have not changed at all, whether you are in the more traditional markets or in those where technology is key. Principally these are as follows:

1. Consumers prefer brands

Brands will continue to be popular among and be preferred by consumers to ordinary products and services. In particular, brands provide customers with:

- *Clear-cut choices*: One's experience of a brand makes the next choice that much easier, both in terms of brand affinity and brand disposition. In the former, a consumer who identifies with Cartier jewelers will pay a premium to wear its jewelry even if the design is widely available elsewhere. In the case of brand disposition, we might get DHL to courier our packages to Hong Kong, but we will never fail to FedEx our documents to Murfreesboro in Tennessee, in the United States.
- *Less confusion*: Brands stand out in the clutter of the marketplace, enabling consumers to choose on the strength of the brand name when product features and benefits are much the same. Consumers will more likely buy a new range of Sony diskettes than buy Sunny diskettes.
- *Greater security*: Powerful brands are always based on quality performance. Hence, people equate brands with a certain level of performance and quality standards. When people choose a certain brand, they are relatively safe in the knowledge that the brand will perform to their expectations. Made to choose between two untried but similarly priced brands of facial cleansers, purchasers are likely to select the brand Kleenex as opposed to Paseo.
- *An emotional dimension*: Brands add an emotional component to the customer relationship and can become "friends" with the consumer. This is probably why some brands are more successful than others in niche areas. For example, though you may be an

ardent fan of Burger King's BK Broiler, you might order and eat a
Fillet-O-Fish at McDonald's when out with the children.

- *Something they can trust*: Powerful brands are built on trust. This
means that people know that what they are buying will live up to
their expectations.

2. Anything can be branded

It is not just companies, products, and services that can be branded, but
people, nations, and ideas too. The object of a branding process is
immaterial, as the same principles apply. For instance, personalities like
Madonna, Tom Cruise, Tina Turner, Tony Blair, and Larry King have all
experienced success at the hands of brand practitioners, while nations are
now also putting their energies behind the branding process. In the book
Branding in Asia (John Wiley & Sons, 2000), Britain and the New
Zealand All Blacks Rugby team are cited as brands that are not products
and services in the traditional branding sense.

In the Digital Age, more emphasis will be put on branding ideas. The
Internet is concerned with information and knowledge, and ideas are
fundamental to its development. Just as the marketing of a product takes
on many guises, brand experience can be fulfilled online through creative
and interactive segments. A static screen shot of Celine Dion may do
absolutely nothing to convince visitors to buy her albums online.
However, if visitors are allowed to view personal snippets of Dion—at
home, in the gym, or in a recording studio—or to check out the various
tour costumes she has worn, a different kind of brand relationship could
develop, and consequently, a new audience segment will emerge.

3. Principles of brand building remain the same

Many successful brands are constructed by developing an identity (often
a brand personality) and positioning this in the minds of the target
audience. A brand identity can be immensely powerful, as many of the
world's top brands have shown. But if not carefully thought through, and
if promises are not delivered, identities sometimes do not correspond

with their images in the marketplace. Adjustments will then have to be made. In some cases the adjustments are major.

For instance, in the 1999 U.S. presidential run-up, Al Gore hired a feminist, Naomi Wolf, to help him become more appealing to women and young voters alike. She insisted that he would have to change the perceptions of voters by appearing more as the "alpha male," and rescind his current image as a "beta-male," whatever these words meant. At the same time, U.S. Republican presidential candidate John McCain, who was known to have a volcanic temper, tried to position himself as a man of integrity and seriousness.

The point is that you should not try to be what you cannot achieve. Branding, particularly positioning, always offers a promise. If you cannot deliver on that promise, you will lose credibility.

4. Brands avoid the commodity trap and offer differentiation

The branding process creates a unique identity for whatever is being branded, offering the advantage of differentiation, which enables the product to stand out from the crowd. Thus, companies find that they can achieve premium prices for what, in many cases, are only ordinary products. For example, Nike apparently has had in some of its operations a production cost of US$2 per pair of shoes, but sells them at well over US$100 per pair all over the world. In some countries, when the price of Mercedes-Benz cars goes up, the waiting list grows longer.

5. Positioning determines brand success

Because differentiation is necessary to brand success, the positioning of all brands is critically important. It has to appeal to separate target audiences. As positioning is the set of techniques used to manage the perceptions of different target audiences, it is a vital part of the branding process. All too often, however, companies do not recognize its true place in corporate strategy. Sometimes companies throw a lot of money at repositioning themselves to appeal to different target audiences, or to improve their brand image with current audiences.

For example, Toyota is actively trying to reach a younger audience and to throw off its rather staid and middle-aged image. In a full-page print advertisement entitled "Passion Road," the copy beneath a picture of a young woman in trainers keeping pace with a car went as follows:

> "Conformity has its comforts. But if you enjoy being independent and like living life to the fullest, it's probably not for you. We know just how you feel. Some people think of Toyota as a rather conservative company. After all, we've been building reliable, high-quality cars for so long, we've become something of a standard. In fact, we're as passionate about life as you are. And we build our cars so we can share that passion with you. That's what the Passion Road is all about. It's a road we travel together . . . a road that is always changing, always challenging . . . a road that inspires a passion for life, and for the future. So if you believe in living life to the fullest, it's time to take another good look at Toyota. And travel with us to the future, and on the Toyota Passion Road."

At the bottom of the advertisement is a panel showing Toyota's sponsorship of the 1999 Asian Games Qualifier. This print advertisement is just one small part of an integrated communications campaign aimed at younger people. Toyota's proposed entry into Formula One racing in the next two or three years will step up the company's investment and brand communications expenditure in making its image more exciting and youth-oriented. (Chapter 4 deals with positioning strategies for hi-tech business in more depth.)

6. Emotion is a key constituent

Emotion sells. The power brands know this full well. They are in fact experts at building emotion into the brand–consumer relationship. The human brain is made up of left and right hemispheres, which work together but have different functions. If a brand can appeal to both sides of the brain, there is a much greater chance that people will buy the brand. In branding, emotion is especially useful where issues such as quality and cost no longer exist. Taking McDonald's as an example, we know it consistently serves quality food in a fast and friendly manner in a clean environment. This, however, is not its brand appeal. The brand appeal of McDonald's lies in whetting the appetites of young children, a hard-to-please segment, with parents eager for a dinner solution in a friendly atmosphere.

There is a great temptation for hi-tech companies to concentrate on promoting their innovative products and services, and to focus on their features and attributes while neglecting to build the brand. This appeal to the rational part of consumer minds is not enough. Hi-tech companies need to learn more about branding with emotion from the traditional consumer goods companies in this respect. (Building brands is discussed later in this chapter.)

7. The brand experience is critical

Brands are only as good as the experience they give to the consumer. One bad experience with a brand can make it lose a customer forever. Giving customers less than their expectation will inevitably lead to a poor brand image. It is therefore important that the brand promise gets delivered. The creative execution of the brand—whether by advertising, logo, or copy—is really only the tip of the iceberg. What makes a brand is every contact every customer has with the company, the product and service quality, the speed of logistics and service recovery, the packaging and display, the feel of the store or site, and the emotional associations that the customer has with the brand.

Powerful brands come from powerful experiences, and nothing is going to change that fact. Even in the world of the Internet, it is as well to remember that to the person logging on, the site is your brand, and every experience he gets when visiting your site will impact on your brand image. As a general rule, consumers evaluate products and services along the lines of the value they get. If it only takes one online experience to serve as a standard for your decision making, a bad site visit may just seal the fate of your brand, even if the visitor has not tried the actual product or service. With the Web as a platform for quick information, one can only imagine the speed it takes for a word—good or bad—to reach others. (See Chapter 6 for information on what makes a good Internet brand experience.)

8. Corporate branding leads the way

The trend of the last few decades in branding has been to leverage the corporate brand. This trend has accelerated in the last ten years or so with the advent of brand valuation techniques and the success of umbrella and house branding. Product branding is less fashionable now, for reasons given elsewhere in this book. Even Procter & Gamble is now concentrating more on leveraging the corporate brand name. For technology branding, the company brand is preferable because it allays the inherent fears some consumers have of technology and technology products. A reliable company name gives strength to the product brands. (Corporate branding is covered later in this chapter.)

9. Brand management is vital

Brands have to be nurtured and managed very carefully, with consistency and appropriateness being the most important elements. Technology brands are no exception to this rule, and it is safe to say that any brand that is not managed well will never enjoy long-term success. Managing the brand is vital in the world of technology, as the speed of change militates against consistency, the key ingredient of brand building.

For organizations that depict themselves as consumer-centric, capabilities within the service value chain must now include online services. The ability to save time on the Internet and the convenience of downloading information, for example, have become part of customer expectations.

What has changed in the world of branding?

Despite all of the above elements that have tended to remain fairly constant, there are some significant changes in branding that hi-tech companies need to know.

1. Brand success can be rapid

Whereas brands used to take decades to develop their strength, they can now be a powerful force in just a few years. Intel Corporation turned from being a loss-making company in the mid-1980s to a megabrand in the 1990s. And we all know about the rapid rise of e-brands such as Amazon.com and others that have gained power brand status in only a few years, mainly by being the first to go into the market. Because of the time compression for branding success, particularly on the Internet, there is now a mad dash to be the number one in each category. Brand building, therefore, now has to be fast, as the rush to get into the hi-tech markets is unprecedented, and differentiation essential.

2. The brand value chain is sometimes shortened

Disintermediation is often used in the context of e-commerce. While true disintermediation is not happening on a widespread basis (only where the middleman sometimes gets knocked out of the loop), a shift in the type of intermediary is developing in the online branding business.

Due to the Internet's mode of presentation, content, process, and style have been compressed and, in some cases, presented as a whole on the screen. The brand proposition and benefits are now delivered through multiple levels in a single interface. It is not surprising that accountability and transparency have come to represent extensions of the brand, and extend to capabilities in information accuracy and timeliness, product pricing, and availability.

3. Segmentation is somewhat different

Customer groups are changing in nature, as traditional forms of segmentation are becoming less important as the digital world advances. For example, the old ways of segmenting markets, such as demographics, have limited value on the Internet, because the communities that are developing on the Net are not constrained by age, income levels, or location. Communities of consumers on the Net have yet to be clearly defined even as new segments are still emerging, such as the Net generation. But the nature of the Web, with its millions of sites, has grouped consumers by the benefits they seek—for example, holiday-makers with interests that vary from spa vacations to business travel to recreational getaways.

4. Mass customization is a brand reality

One of the most powerful changes the technological revolution has brought to marketing is the ability, through sophisticated software, to talk to customers and customize offerings to them one at a time. Treating each person differently is what marketers had only dreamed of. Not anymore, as mass customization is now a reality. Sites on the Internet that employ such dedicated applications include Amazon.com and Pets.com. (See Chapter 4 for a discussion on mass customization and one-to-one marketing.)

5. The nature of the consumer experience has changed

While brand experience remains the key to brand popularity, the nature of that experience has changed somewhat. The full impact of this change has yet to be seen, but already firms are realizing, some at a cost, that consumers want different things. (Chapter 6 looks at how you can successfully brand your company on the Net.)

6. The roles of advertising, promotion, and public relations have changed

The nature of the impact of technology, particularly the Internet, on the traditional forms of brand communication, such as advertising and public relations, is currently being hotly debated. But some notable trends are occurring now. These are discussed in detail in Chapter 3.

7. Size is no longer important

In the past, size was the name of the game in creating a global brand. Mass marketing meant mass distribution. Companies had to develop distribution power and manufacturing capacity across many continents.

Today, these are no longer necessary. In fact, smaller companies operating from their home base can achieve global recognition without recourse to traditional distribution channels. On the Internet, a company can look really good without having a physical presence. Branding creates that image.

8. Brand loyalty is harder to get and maintain

Customer loyalty is increasingly becoming significant as people become more choosy and assert their right to choose. This is particularly true on the Internet where, if customers do not get instant gratification, a click will send them quickly to another site that could give them what they want. Internet users, according to research, are less loyal than traditional shoppers. Customer relationship management (CRM) is becoming more important in the battle for brand loyalty, and technology is the catalyst for success in this field, as illustrated in Chapter 5.

9. Brands have financial value

Brand valuation is not new, but it is only recently that it has become more sophisticated and accepted. It is now arguably the most captivating part of brand building. In some parts of the world, brands are now included in company balance sheets as assets in their own right. They can be used to leverage corporate worth, and as collateral for loans. An illustration of brand value is Vodaphone's takeover of Air Touch. The market valuation of Air Touch was US$45 billion, but Vodaphone paid US$60 billion for it, a premium of US$15 billion. Still another example is that of Britain's Orange. Coming late into the market as a highly priced player in 1994, the mobile phone operator's estimated brand value, according to ABN Amro, was £200 million after only three years of operation. This year it was sold for £31 billion. Finally, in Hong Kong, VTech paid US$115 million in the first quarter of 2000 to acquire the rights to the AT&T brand name for ten years, in addition to making royalty payments. (More information is given on this interesting topic in Chapter 8.)

THE PRINCIPLES OF BRANDING

Before we look at specific brand techniques, it is worthwhile to outline the basic principles involved in branding—the things that underpin brand success. These principles of branding, applied with great success around the world by the power brands, are just as applicable to technology companies and products. In fact, technology enterprises, products, and services need the skills of branding even more than the ordinary, prestige, and luxury consumer brands that we know so well. We shall discuss the reasons for this claim later. For now, we will take a look at what a brand is, and how the world's most powerful brands develop the strength and influence that generate global success.

Why are brands important to consumers?

Brands are important to consumers because they provide them with:

- choice
- a means of simplifying decisions
- quality assurance
- risk avoidance
- self-expression

Brands provide choices

People like to have choices, and brands give them the freedom to choose. As markets fragment more and more, companies are finding it necessary to give different consumer segments different choices. Brands can provide choices, allowing consumers to differentiate between the various company offerings. If we step into a consumer electronics shop, we will be amazed by the rows and rows of television sets, video players, and other products. The amount of variations in each product range is as bewildering as the amount of companies offering the products. In this kind of situation, people gravitate toward brands. Brand names provide us with choices, making the decision-making process so much easier.

Brands simplify decisions

Brands make the decision to buy easier. A person may not know a lot about every product he is interested in, but a brand does make it easier for him to choose. People can decide more quickly if they recognize brands, making their lives easier. Brand recognition is especially important to technology products, as people do not usually understand all the technical aspects of what they are buying. And as product parity increases, brands simplify the decision as to which product to buy. Well-known brands get more attention than relatively unknown ones, partly because they are familiar, and mainly because they are trusted.

Brands provide quality assurance

Consumers will choose quality products and services wherever and whenever they can. Once they experience a brand, they automatically equate this experience with a certain degree of quality. A pleasant experience makes for a good brand recall. Hence, consumers will gravitate toward brands that they know provide high quality standards. Experiencing different brands helps consumers to compare quality standards and to know what value they are getting for their money.

Brands facilitate risk avoidance

Most consumers are risk-averse. They do not want to buy products, particularly technology goods, if they have the slightest doubt about their performance. An experience of a brand, if positive, gives consumers reassurance and comfort in purchasing even expensive items. Trust is one of the most important factors in why people buy certain technology products and not others. Brands build trust, and great brands are well trusted.

Brands provide a means of self-expression

Brands generate opportunities for people to express themselves in many different ways. They can help people to express, among other socio-psychological needs, their:

- social status
- success
- aspirations
- love and friendship
- personality

Wearing a Piaget watch, for instance, means more than just displaying an expensive fashion accessory, while driving a VW Beetle could give one an insight into the owner's thoughts and feelings. Buying a personal computer with a Pentium 3 chip means more than just a bit more processing power to many people. Brands enable people to express themselves, what they think, what they value and love, their lifestyles, and their dreams. Brands exist in people's minds, and sometimes speak more than words do.

Critical to brand development—understanding the target audience

Critical to any branding process is a precise understanding of the brand's target customers. As good consumer insight is essential, consumer profiling has become an integral part of brand development and management. Companies like Harley-Davidson built their brands on a thorough understanding of how their potential and actual customers think, feel, and behave. Harley-Davidson spent a great deal of time following bikers around on weekends to find out their thoughts and feelings about biking. The result was a profile of the people who loved big bikes, coupled with an underlying knowledge of the sense of freedom that biking gave them. There is no substitute for getting inside consumers' minds, which helps companies build a brand personality that conforms to the target audience.

What is a brand?

Many companies have learned, to their sorrow, that brands are not just trademarks, products, logos, symbols, or names. The millions of dollars companies spend on corporate identity projects are often wasted because there is no brand strategy behind them. Thus, consumers experience the same dull and irritating service, mediocre or sub-quality product, and a less-than-satisfactory customer experience. Similarly, having a good name does not guarantee success, as companies like Ford found out with products like the Edsel many years ago. Many other companies have placed their faith in the advertising dollar, hoping that mass communications will do the trick. There are still many that do not realize that all of these elements are necessary but not sufficient to produce a great brand.

One of the most useful comments on the difference between mere products and brands is attributed to Stephen King, who said:

> "A product is something that's made in a factory, a brand is something bought by consumers. A product can be copied by a competitor, a brand is unique. A product can be quickly outdated; a successful brand, properly managed, can be timeless."

People like King have made sure that the skills of branding are getting due recognition, while many companies are now trying to emulate the successes of the world's best brands. The most powerful brands, which have become household names, were developed by the establishment of unique brand characters or personalities, the achievement of strong positions in consumer minds through consistent and appropriate communications, and by providing good quality and a memorable customer experience. Before we look at how brands are built, let us look briefly at product and service elements.

THE ELEMENTS OF PRODUCTS AND SERVICES

Features and attributes

When we look at any product being sold to us, we will likely focus on its features and attributes. The focus becomes even more pronounced with technology products. We might be looking at the size of computer memory, the power of the chip, the speaker quality, and the size of the woofers in a hi-fi system. These things are important in the world of technology, because technology is all about the latest and most innovative features available.

Practical benefits

Technology for the sake of technology has little value to the consumer. To be sure, consumers are interested in technological features, but what they like to know more than these are the benefits that they can get from a product's technical specifications. Having a gear change system on a car steering wheel is not just a trendy, new idea; to many people it gives the benefit of safety through its ability to keep both hands on the wheel; to others, however, it represents convenience.

Intangible benefits and value

Technological features can also bring about benefits that have more emotional value, which helps the sales process. Going back to the example of the steering wheel gear change, some customers transform into Formula One drivers when they sit in the driving seat! In their minds they are able to live out their dreams by pretending to be Mikka Hakkinen (or Michael Schumacher, if you like) using the same technology as their heroes.

The value of the most successful brands goes beyond their features and benefits. It is of an intangible kind, as it adds personality to their products and services, which in turn appeals to the emotional side of consumers. Therein lies one of the secrets of their success. Technology companies would do well to focus more on this intangible element, because people will always like the human touch. After all, emotion always sells.

Adding personality to your product or service can be done in various ways, as explained below.

How brands are built

Brands are built by creating a strong brand personality, or a set of brand values, and creating a favorable perception of the brand in the minds of the target audience. Figure 1 presents brand building in a simplified diagrammatic form.

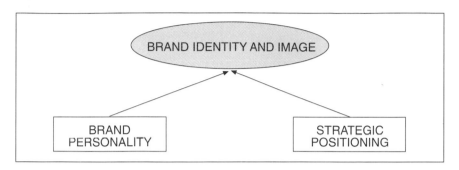

Figure 1: How to build a brand

Corporate identity, brand identity, and brand image

It is important to distinguish between corporate identity, brand identity, and brand image. Corporate identity is concerned with the visual aspects of a company's presence. When companies undertake corporate identity exercises, they are usually modernizing their visual image in terms of logo, design, and collaterals. Such efforts do not normally entail a change in brand values so that the heart of the brand remains the same—what it stands for, or its personality. Unfortunately, many companies do not realize this fallacy, as they are sometimes led to believe by agencies and consultancy companies that the visual changes will change the brand image. But changes to logos, signage, and even outlet design do not always change consumer perceptions of quality, service, and the intangible associations that come to the fore when the brand name is seen or heard.

The best that such changes can do is to reassure consumers that the company is concerned about how it looks. Brands do have to maintain a modern look, and the visual identity needs to change over time. But the key to successfully effecting a new look is evolution, not revolution. Totally changing the brand visuals can give rise to consumer concerns about changes of ownership, or possible changes in brand values, or even unjustified extravagance. If there is a strong brand personality to which consumers are attracted, then substantial changes may destroy emotional attachments to the brand. People do not expect or like wild swings in the personality and behavior of other people, and they are just as concerned when the brands to which they have grown used exhibit similar "schizophrenic" changes.

On the other hand, if the intention is to substantially improve the standing of the brand, then corporate identity changes can be accompanied by widespread changes to organizational culture, quality, and service standards. If done well, and if consumers experience a great new or improved experience, then the changes will, over the longer term, have a corresponding positive effect on brand image. If you are spending a vast amount of money on corporate identity, it is as well to remember this.

Brand identity is the total proposition that a company makes to consumers—the promise it makes. It may consist of features and attributes, benefits, performance, quality, service support, and the values that the brand possesses. As we shall see in the next chapter, the brand can be viewed as a product, a personality, a set of values, and a position it occupies in people's minds. Brand identity is everything the company wants the brand to be seen as.

Brand image, on the other hand, is the totality of consumer perceptions about the brand, or how they see it, which may not coincide with the brand identity. Companies have to work hard on the consumer experience to make sure that what customers see and think is what they want them to.

Achieving harmony between brand identity and brand image

Many companies do not spend enough time or effort in making sure that the identity they want their brand to have (desired consumer perceptions) matches the image of the brand (actual consumer perceptions). One potential problem that can arise here is a lack of credibility, especially if the brand identity, or proposition, offers something that it cannot deliver. Whenever companies make certain promises to consumers through brand communications, they should ensure that they keep those promises, and that the consumer experience reinforces them.

Having made those important distinctions, we can now turn to how powerful brands are built, and how the brand promise is created. The first step is the creation of a brand personality for the product, service, or company. The positioning of the brand is explained briefly after this, and in more detail in Chapter 4.

Using brand personality to develop a brand

A key question related to brand personality is, "What does the brand stand for?" As mentioned above, world-class companies answer this question by creating a brand identity, but what makes a great brand identity is a good set of brand values. These values are often, although not always, used to form a distinctive brand personality or character. (In brand lexicon, these two words are often used interchangeably.) The development of brand personality is a technique used by many of the world's leading companies in developing their brands.

The power brands of this world do not create personalities for their companies, products, and services by chance. They realize that personality makes for differentiation or uniqueness. Moreover, they have research at their disposal that tells them that consumers readily identify with personality characteristics when they encounter them via communications media. The overriding importance of brand personality is that consumers understand it so easily. As people are used to daily encounters with other human beings, and to picking up communication signals from others, they are quick to respond to a personality that is projected by a brand, be it a product, service, or company.

In the Harley-Davidson example mentioned above, the resulting personality of the brand following the company's research into the lives of bikers is best described by these words:

- male
- macho
- patriotic
- proud of heritage
- loves freedom

This brand personality so summed up the personality of the bikers the company was aiming to please that a failed, outdated, and unprofitable brand was transformed into a successful, outstanding, and profitable one. The concept of brand personality is discussed further in Chapter 3.

Matching brands to consumers

What Harley-Davidson did was to cleverly match the brand personality to that of its prospective customer group. Companies that are experienced in branding actually research their target audiences and build personalities to match the characteristics that typify the customer base, and which they admire or aspire to.

Developing friendship

At the root of building brands using personality is the need to tap into everyone's desire to have a friend or a meaningful relationship. Brands can develop emotional associations in people's minds, which are just as powerful as the emotional feelings they have for people. They can become symbols of many things. The book *Branding in Asia* enumerates what brands can symbolize to people:

- what they stand for
- what they believe in
- what they care about
- what they love
- what they aspire to be
- the type of person they want to be with
- the kind of relationship they want
- what they want people to know about them
- the kind of friend they want

For these and many other reasons, people express themselves through brands, and rely on them. In this way, brand personality strengthens the brand–customer relationship through the development of powerful emotional appeals.

Positioning brands to make a difference

Brand positioning is one of the central issues affecting branding in technology-based companies. When it is difficult to gain a sustainable competitive advantage in product features and benefits, how do you manage the perceptions of consumers to get them to think that your company or product is different and better? If a company cannot explain why it or its products are different and better, then it will have survival problems. If it can answer these questions to the satisfaction of its consumers, then it will attract and retain good consumers. The answers to these questions lie in the positioning strategy or strategies that a company adopts for its brand. Positioning is critical to technology companies and products, as it is very difficult to gain differentiation through easily copied features and attributes. Chapter 4 addresses this subject in detail.

Choosing the brand level

One of the decisions that companies have to make when creating and managing brands is the kind of branding they want to have, specifically the level of branding. Companies have basically three options when choosing the level of branding they need to adopt:

a) product branding
b) corporate branding
c) house or endorsement branding

In practice, these three levels exist as part of a continuum, and companies can choose many variations to suit their needs. Following is a discussion of the differences between the three.

Product branding

Strictly speaking, product branding is where a company decides that the product should stand on its own, and be left to succeed or fail without any support from the corporate brand or company name. Fast-moving consumer goods are traditionally associated with this level of branding, such as Lux soap. Companies that are well known for product branding are Procter & Gamble and Unilever. Both are currently cutting down on the number of brands in their portfolios. In the case of Unilever, the number is to be reduced from 1,600 to 400. Procter & Gamble currently has a global strategy to start leveraging the corporate brand.

While the product branding emanating from excellent companies like these two has long been admired, there are few advantages to branding each product separately and having little attachment between the company name and the brands. It is expensive, and denies the individual brands access to the strength of the corporate brand name. Nowadays the trend is very much toward corporate branding, or branding where the corporate name appears with the product brand.

Corporate branding

In the extreme case of corporate branding, the company gets all of the limelight and there is no mention of products and services at all, as with Amazon.com. In other instances, products are relegated to perhaps just a set of letters and numbers, examples being the BMW 3, 5, and 7 series models, the Audi A6, and the Nokia 8 series. In these examples, however, the corporate brand is paramount and lends all its identity to the products concerned. Products in return derive strength from the parent brand values, while individual brands share the same marketing communications very easily, reducing overall costs significantly compared to product branding.

House or endorsement branding

House branding (or endorsement branding, as it is also known) is the most popular brand level among companies. In this compromise area, firms try to get the best of both worlds by allowing each product to have its own brand name while using the corporate brand name alongside it. Examples are Porsche Boxster S, the Intel Pentium range, and Microsoft Windows. Companies, of course, can try a variety of combinations, such as putting the firm's name before the product name, as the three examples above illustrate, and giving the product name the main mention with the corporate name as the sign-off.

In technology industries, the corporate brand name lends strength to products and services. With the introduction of the Pentium chip by Intel Corporation, for example, the company felt that the product brand name would sum up the benefits of the offering more easily, giving consumers a kind of shorthand, which was more meaningful to them. But it was also deemed essential to have the Intel name precede the product brand name, if only to allay the fears of people about the performance of critical and complex products. A Pentium chip introduced without the Intel house brand would probably have been much less successful. Hewlett-Packard felt this way about its products' prospects for success when it found out that if they removed the company brand name from their product lines, such as LaserJet and DeskJet, they would stand to lose up to half their potential sales!

A brand is a promise of an experience

Whatever makes up a brand, and however this is communicated to the people it is intended for, the success or failure of a brand depends upon the experience the consumer gets from it. The brand in reality is the experience. What it all boils down to is that a brand is a promise to the consumer of what your product, service, or company stands for, and of the kind of experience they can get from it. That promise has to be delivered.

The result of good branding is an experience that delights customers, and one that is good enough to keep them coming back. This is true whether the brand is a product, a service, or a company. But the customer experience is a function of value. The value that consumers find in brands can be both tangible and intangible. It is often the intangible values that attach people to a particular brand rather than another. With technology products, performance represents a large part of the value. But as consumers tend to be a bit fearful of technology, it is often the brand name that adds the element of trust. The trust factor inherent in the brand name is the intangible value of the brand, and where there is little difference in the performance of technology products, this is the differentiating factor and gets the sale.

Consider the example of Delta Dental Plan whose excellent guarantee program has attracted thousands of new clients while effectively retaining existing ones, thanks to its commitment to keeping its promises.

Delta Dental Plan—keeping promises

Since Delta Dental Plan of Massachusetts instituted its Guarantee of Service Excellence Program in 1990, it has gained 364,000 new customers, which translate to an additional US$162 million in revenue. Delta Dental's guarantee program promises—and delivers—cash payments when the company fails to meet the high standards of that program. The first step to developing the program involved identifying what customers wanted from their dental insurance company. Delta Dental conducted research and focus group discussions with companies requiring the services of dental insurance firms. The result was a list of seven guarantees, each broken down into two areas: the service and the refund.

For example, if the service is not provided, the client receives a refund. If Delta Dental does not provide a complete and accurate identification card for each subscriber within 15 calendar days, it will pay the group US$25 per identification card. Another service guarantee states that the company will resolve a customer's question immediately by phone, or guarantee the customer an initial update within one business day and continuous follow-up through to resolution. If it does not, it will pay the group US$50 per occurrence. An important element in the success of the program, however, is that the company did not implement it until it had thoroughly trained every employee in service procedures and service philosophy.

Delta Dental president Robert Hunter said employee dedication to excellence is an "extremely effective competitive advantage." He knew that making empty promises would be an exercise in futility, as customers would soon realize that Delta Dental was paying only lip service to customer service. By putting its money where its mouth is, however, the company not only has retained customers, it has attracted thousands of new customers. Its market share has increased by 40%, while 1997 revenues rose to US$280 million. To say that the results of Delta Dental's guarantee program have been impressive would be an understatement. During the first nine months of the program, Delta Dental budgeted US$75,000 for refunds; it paid out only US$1,610. During the first year of the program, the company reported an average cost saving of 15%; it had anticipated only 10%. The company also exceeded its expectations in processing claims within 15 days. It had promised 85% but actually achieved 98%. (*Source: John Tschohl, Service Quality Institute.*)

Summary

This chapter has identified the main elements of brand importance and brand building. Although the information it contains is general in nature, everything you have read so far applies to technology branding. In Chapter 3, we will look at technology branding closely, and examine the techniques most appropriate for the building of brands for technology companies and products.

In the meantime, the following case study illustrates the depth of thinking and orchestration that has to go into a good branding program.

CASE STUDY

BUICK FROM SHANGHAI GM
Building and launching a brand in a new market

Shanghai General Motors is a joint venture between General Motors and Shanghai Automotive Industry Corporation formed in 1995. As a US$1.52-billion investment, it was the largest ever Sino-American joint venture in China. It set out to build a new automotive company in China, with a new facility, new brand, new product technology, and a high degree of localization in all aspects of the business. This case features the launch campaign of Buick from GM in China, and is an excellent example of how a company starts with research into customer needs and wants, develops key consumer insights, and translates these into a well-thought-through integrated communications campaign, based on a solid brand platform. Within 12 months, Shanghai GM moved from being virtually unknown in its market segment to enjoying segment leadership.

Consumer insight

One of the issues facing the company was that neither the joint ventures that existed at the time nor the local companies had lived up to the expectations of Chinese consumers, who were highly skeptical of locally made automotive products. The company quickly learned that consumers expected world-class automotive products and service.

The launch campaign goals

The launch of Buick from Shanghai GM had two main aims:

1. To build high expectations about Buick quality and service as distinct from other local products in the market
2. To position Shanghai GM as a forward-looking company, leading the reform and development of the China automobile industry, which was a responsible choice for the customers.

The brand personality

The brand values for Buick, in the form of personality characteristics, were:

- leadership
- trustworthiness
- respectability
- accessibility
- ability to discern

And while these were the subject of internal education for the company, work was also going on to educate consumers about the characteristics of a world-class car with world-class service.

Phase 1 of the campaign

The twin aims of the first brand communications campaign were to build an awareness of and interest in the coming of Buick from Shanghai GM, and to create a favorable and trustworthy corporate image for the joint venture. The campaign consisted of one 60-second corporate image TV commercial. Three versions of print ads and two versions of outdoor advertisements together portrayed Shanghai GM as a different kind of corporation, determined to set new standards for the Chinese auto industry through invincible teamwork. The powerful TV commercial used a mature male voice-over proclaiming, "It is not just a car, it is a spirit. Making Buick with the spirit of today's Generation. Buick from Shanghai GM."

Phase one of the campaign also launched the Web site www.shanghaigm.com, the first automobile online site in China, which served as an effective marketing and distribution tool to facilitate two-way interactive dialogue with customers.

Phase 2 of the campaign

The aim of this phase was to build consumer belief that Shanghai GM was different and better than other joint-venture auto manufacturers in China. Providing a detailed elaboration of the Spirit of Today's Generation at work in Shanghai GM, the phase was characterized by a series of five print ads providing vivid descriptions of the attitudes and team spirit of everybody behind Buick from Shanghai GM—including sales and after-sales service personnel and suppliers of quality parts. The same campaign phase sought to promote the sense of mission and responsibility of the "Buick People"—their pioneering spirit, service quality, and "customer first" attitude.

Phase 3 of the campaign

The launch of the third phase of the campaign supported the commercial launch. The message was, "No compromise on quality. The Spirit of Today's Generation." This slogan successfully addressed the need of

Chinese customers for a world-class car. The print ad series was perfectly complementary to the TV commercial, providing a different perspective on the superior product features and consumer benefits of Buick from Shanghai GM.

In addition to the above campaigns, the company provided Facilities Environment Design for retail and after-sales partners, full sales support programs, and the most comprehensive customer relationship management program in China.

What Shanghai GM did is one of the best examples we have come across of how a company can build a brand quickly in a new and foreign market, using all the elements of the brand–building process. Aside from market success, the company also won an international award for brand building.

Shanghai GM's campaign plan outline is shown in Figure 2.

The Campaign Structure

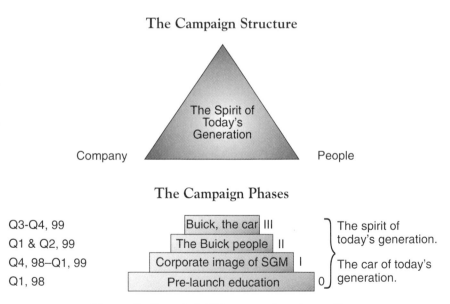

Figure 2: Shanghai GM's campaign plan outline

3

Branding and Technology

This chapter presents the critical aspects of branding for technology companies and products. It reinforces the fact that traditional consumer branding has a lot to offer hi-tech companies, and focuses on the critical aspects of the branding process. It takes into account the problems that hi-tech companies face in marketing their products in a fast-changing world, and presents a framework for effective technology branding.

BRANDING IN THE WORLD OF TECHNOLOGICAL PARITY

Branding is increasingly becoming important. Just ask consumer goods companies, which have learned how much value skillful branding can add to products and services, and how it can transform ordinary commodities into highly prestigious products and services. When all is said and done, marketing in the new century comes down to the search for differentiation in what is increasingly turning out to be a world of parity. Branding makes that difference.

Technology is particularly vulnerable to parity exposure, as it is readily available to any firm that wants it. Even breakthrough technology provides only a short-term competitive advantage; technology products can be copied with ease; features and benefits of technology products are more or less standard. So what will make one product stand out from the crowd?

Consider this example. Two new identical electronic products are simultaneously introduced to the marketplace. There is no difference in their prices or features. Functionally, the products are identical, offering the same standards of performance and warranties. But one of the products carries a company brand name you have not heard of, while the other is made by Sony. Assuming you want to buy one of these products, which will you choose? Not a difficult decision, is it? In the age of similarity, branding makes the difference.

Surprisingly, technology companies, in general, have not adopted branding with the same enthusiasm as those companies delivering fast-moving consumer goods. One of the reasons for this appears to be that many top managers of technology-based companies are not marketing specialists and therefore do not have branding skills. As a result, they sometimes find it difficult to accept that consumer value is often based on intangibles such as emotional associations, as opposed to hard, tangible facts like product features. They are more concerned with designing and producing innovative products that outperform the competition, rather than building long-term brand relationships.

Apart from the mental set problem, there are other more fundamental problems associated with marketing technology products that make brand development more difficult for managers in technology companies. These have to do mainly with general consumer behavior toward technology products and the lack of response by technology companies to these concerns. One of these is the turbulent and accelerating world of change that hi-tech managers operate in.

Consistency versus change

One of the difficulties inherent in branding technology has to do with the nature of technology itself. Traditional branding, as we know it with, say, fast-moving consumer goods, has delivered success through consistency and appropriateness of product, brand identity, and execution. The top brands of the 1920s in many categories are still the leading brands today, like Colgate, Kodak, and Kellogg's. These power brands have shown that consistency is key to brand building. The Coca-Cola formula is essentially the same today as it was 100 years ago. What is more, the swirling Coca-Cola bottle still dominates the brand's packaging and advertising. Colgate has broadened the appeal of the brand to include flavors and additives but nevertheless remains essentially the same. Marlboro is another power brand that has demonstrated amazing consistency in its brand communications, with over 40 years of advertising and promotion that focuses precisely on the brand personality attributes of strength and independence.

When it comes to technology products, the difficulty lies in product consistency, because change is the name of the game. The rapid developments in technology mean equally fast developments in technology products. With product life cycles down to just a matter of weeks, some companies aspire to introduce two or three new products per month. Given this scenario, companies find it difficult to provide the consistency required to give consumers the security they want in a brand. Worse still, consumers have a built-in resistance to and distrust of technology products—which cannot quite be said of traditional consumer products. Consequently, their buying behavior tends to be different also.

The technology buyer's decision-making style

The approach of people who buy technology products is different from that of buyers of traditional consumer goods. Firstly, technology products are by their very nature more complex, besides being generally more expensive. Thus, buyers have to study the products more carefully before buying them.

Secondly, there is the issue of the buyer's background. Businesses account for the majority of purchases of technology products, whereas individuals make up the majority of those of who buy consumer products. This situation is changing, of course, as technology becomes more and more a part of our everyday lives. Still, business purchases are more likely to undergo careful scrutiny.

Thirdly, as mentioned above, the life cycles of consumer products tend to be longer than those of technology products, which sometimes take just a few weeks, depending on the market situation. The home PC life cycle, for example, "is very short, about eight to ten weeks," said James Radford, director of consumer business group for Hewlett-Packard in India. "So inventory has to move. Consumers want new features every time. Today speed to market is extremely important," he added. This is the case with the developing markets where, in the PC world, most of the purchases are of the cheaper unbranded products. But in the more developed markets, constant innovation makes the decision-making process more difficult. Buyers, especially ordinary consumers, are reluctant to rush in and buy, thinking that the product they intend to purchase could become obsolete before they even get accustomed to using it.

Lastly, but by no means the least, many consumers of technology products have innate fears about what they buy. One such fear is that the product they are buying may not deliver on its promises. They are therefore concerned about product performance. Fantastic features are attractive to some, "but will they work?" This is a question they often find themselves asking. More to the point, "Do I really need them?" asks the consumer. With manufacturers offering little in the way of long-term warranties, such fears can easily give rise to consumer reluctance and remove the impulse to buy, which is so characteristic of fast-moving consumer goods. Then, too, they are often "technophobic," referring to an irrational fear of technology. Machines and gadgets have always fascinated human beings, who also view them with some dose of trepidation, if not skepticism.

Even as companies try to make products that are easy to use, the consumer, based on his experience, still thinks that complex mechanisms can be difficult to operate. Such thoughts come with questions like this: "What happens if I press the wrong button and cause a major problem?" While change is a constant in boardroom discussions and results in change-oriented strategies, the average consumer is still afraid of change and regards the ever-changing world as a threat.

To sum it up, an overriding issue with many technology product buyers is fear, be it utilitarian or psychological in nature. "Will it work?" and "Can I trust it?" are commonly asked questions among consumers. You may have asked yourself the same questions. The main implication of all this for every producer of technology products is that gaining trust is vital to the company's successful marketing of its products. In this respect, the corporate brand has an important role to play.

Here are some of the common traps technology firms fall into in relation to branding.

The feature trap

Technology companies do not help themselves when they concentrate on the promotion of product features and attributes to the exclusion of the brand. This emphasis on features (such as processing speed or capacity) does not elicit an emotional response from the consumer. As mentioned in the previous chapter, it is essential for brand building. Ask yourself this question, "If yours is a technology company, how much of your advertising and promotion budget goes to brand image as opposed to what goes to product sales?" You might be shocked by the answer.

The distribution trap

Similarly, many technology companies concentrate on building distribution channels at the brand's expense. Even among the world's top brands in consumer electronics and personal computers, trying to get decent, fast service out of distribution agents can be a nightmare. Moreover, many appoint distributors who compete in selling the company's brand by giving discounts. In other words, the distributors are carrying out intra-brand competition when they should be concentrating on inter-brand competition. In their efforts to capture global market share, some companies allow their brand to get out of control. They do not control the service quality levels upon which strong brands are made, and do not give incentives to their distributors to represent their brands properly. Powerful brands rely on trust—an element that technology companies need to be more aware of so that they can act accordingly. Building volume does not necessarily build a brand.

The quality trap

It is tempting to focus on quality to the exclusion of everything else. After all, no one wants to buy a product that is of poor quality. In fact, performance and quality are the necessary means of entry into the hi-tech business game. However, concentrating on these factors alone can lead to blind spots. In the early 1980s, Chrysler almost went out of business through its single-minded focus on quality. Resisting entry into the small car market, it said, "You can't fit Chrysler engineering into a small car." So obsessed was Chrysler with its technological competitive advantage that it nearly missed the emerging market changes.

Technology is only an enabler, and business has to have a balance. As such, it is impossible to build a powerful brand without a quality product or service. Your company has to be able to stand up against the competition on this important dimension. But do not forget the other factors that will make consumers buy from your company and not from your competitor.

Branding and consumer trust

As we mentioned, most consumers are risk-averse. Such an attitude is even more pronounced with respect to technology products, which, to the average buyer, represent even more risk than do traditional consumer products. Strong brands address consumer concerns about quality and reliability by gaining the trust of consumers. Trust is therefore where you can find a place for the quality dimension of your business. It is also the reason why Sony, Canon, and other companies have focused on investing in quality over the years, thus strengthening their reputation and developing their brands further. As the late Akio Morita of Sony once said, "I have always believed that the company name is the life of an enterprise. It carries responsibility and guarantees the quality of the product."

In this light, corporate branding is more powerful in helping overcome consumer fears and gaining their trust. Product branding, often associated with fast-moving consumer products such as soaps and detergents, is unlikely to succeed in branding technology products. The corporate name, over time, yields credibility and alleviates the fear of the unknown in highly innovative product markets. Sony, which ventured into product branding with the introduction of the Walkman, still strongly endorsed the product by placing the company brand name before the product name. Other companies, despite having well-known brands, still go to great lengths to reassure the customer about their technology. A Toshiba television commercial, for example, has a sign-off/tag line that says, "Toshiba: Technology You Can Trust."

If the three Cs of traditional branding are consistency, consistency, and consistency, the three Cs of technology are change, change, and change. The success of branding is assured when there is consistency and reinforcement. Technology is tied to change, which militates against strong brand development unless there is a form of consistency that will give consumers some degree of security. People naturally distrust change, and therefore need constant reassurances that the new products before them are reliable. Corporate branding offers this assurance to buyers. Because the name is constant, the consumer can relate to the brand and what the brand stands for even as the products and services change to reflect new technology. In the branding game, trust is everything.

CHANGING THE HI-TECH MANAGEMENT MINDSET

Many top, senior, and middle managers of technology companies have a technical background but not a lot of marketing experience. They have a product—rather than a customer—focus, which is not surprising. Technology companies have a naturally strong product focus; they are what Stan Shih of Acer calls "technology-centric," as opposed to "customer-centric," in their thinking and behavior.

However, the thinking behind such a product orientation can lead not just to a downgrading of the marketing status and branding but also to some serious misunderstandings about the concepts involved and the value of these functions to organizations.

Strategic marketing, in particular branding, has much more to do with a company's success than is often acknowledged in the world of hi-tech products, features, innovations, and rapid change. In his foreword to the book *Branding in Asia*, Shih says it is true that "only innovative technology, products, and services that can provide high quality and value to customers will sustain businesses in the new competitive era." Yet it is an inescapable fact that "brand sells."

Acer Computer aims to become more consumer-oriented and is therefore working hard on shifting its management mindset from being technology-centric to consumer-centric. Aware that the computer industry has always focused on technology, emphasizing products more than people, Acer is repositioning itself to become a customer-centric intellectual property and service company. This effort is signified by its slogan "Acer: Bringing People and Technology Together."

Many other technology-based companies have yet to start making the same transition as Acer, owing mainly to misconceptions, or blind spots, that still characterize much of hi-tech management thinking. These false notions are explained below.

The price/commodity trap

Managers can easily adopt the mindset that price and performance are the drivers of business success in technology companies. One of the reasons behind this thinking is that the ease with which technology products and services can be replicated by competitors leads to a parity situation in many markets. This situation, combined with the fact that technological performance is also very much a level playing field, prompts managers to compete on price and promotional offensives to win the sales battle. Such actions are extremely dangerous, and can easily lead companies into the commodity trap, whereby differentiation on price drives margins lower and lower, and consumers demand more and more of the same. Consumers see less and less value in the brand and increasingly concentrate on price advantages.

Price versus value

The main mindset change managers need is to recognize that price does not equal value in the minds of consumers. Of course, everyone wants good prices, but industry studies show that price influences the buying decision only if a company cannot differentiate itself or its products by any other means.

Companies can add value to their products and services in many ways—that is, through features, warranties, after-sales service, and other things of benefit to the customer. This is particularly true of technology products, where the opportunity to add value is very high. So, value in the minds of people looking to buy hi-tech products involves much more than price—price is just one part of the value equation for them. Value for money is a prime motivator, but when the value element is dissected, many other factors play a large part in consumers' decision to buy.

The problem with these ways of adding value is that they can easily be replicated by every competitor. In other words, they no longer differentiate one company's offer from another. Technology is freely available and easy to put into operation, leaving little time for companies to keep a strategic competitive advantage. Even if they manage to produce something new in the short term, or gain some kind of unique selling proposition, it is unlikely that the product will last more than a few weeks. What, then, constitutes real differentiation and real added value in the minds of consumers? The answer lies in the brand name and what it stands for.

Brand image as a value contributor

In the world of parity, image is everything. In the crowded marketplace, it is the only thing that distinguishes a company or a product from the rest. Without a strong image, it is extremely difficult for a company to acquire new customers and retain existing ones, and at the same time charge premium prices. Power brands manage to achieve all three goals. Many cars, refrigerators, elevators, and computer chips have similar features and performance capabilities, so why do consumers prefer to buy

Mercedes-Benz, Zanussi, Otis, and Intel? The answer again lies in the power of the brand image and what it means to those who patronize the brand.

Image creates huge value. The value of a brand can be quantified in monetary terms, but the real value in the competitive marketplace is the ability of brands to capture consumer attention and influence choice. Brands provide emotional attraction when the rational mind cannot choose, and help allay the fears of consumers concerning technology products.

Building a strong technology brand

For all the reasons discussed above, the developers of technology brands need to build them holistically, considering the brand as a:

- set of values
- person
- symbol
- product
- position
- culture

In this way, companies will overcome the fears surrounding hi-tech products and build brands that are close to the powerful consumer brands that have dominated brand space in their global markets.

The brand as a set of values

It is common knowledge that all successful brands are built around a set of brand values, setting the scene for what the brand stands for. Technology brands are no exception to this rule. However, many companies choose to articulate values revolving around superior quality and performance. This is not surprising when we consider that companies that do not reach high standards in terms of quality and reliability are usually destined for failure. Conversely, data from the Strategic Planning Institute in Cambridge, Massachusetts, shows that companies noted for outstanding quality and service:

- charge prices that are on average 9% higher
- grow twice as fast as the average company
- experience yearly market share increases of 6%, while the average company loses 2% each year
- receive an average return of 12% (the average during the research period was 1% to 2%)

Many successful companies use closely defined brand values to make sure they meet customer expectations, thus avoiding costly mistakes. Quality, for instance, is one of Intel's six core values; Motorola is famous for its six-sigma quality standard. Different companies have different values, depending on what they believe is important to their business. Values counterbalance the numbers side of a business, and lend emotional strength to the corporate culture, giving people a sense of their own destiny.

But quality and operational effectiveness, important though they are, especially for hi-tech companies, are not enough to give consumers reason to pick a brand and stay with it. Brand personality is also important. It is the one thing that technology companies must learn from consumer goods companies. Charles Schwab introduced his own personal values of fairness, respect, continuous improvement, and trust. General Electric (GE) has three values, namely, speed, simplicity, and self-confidence. Both sets of values are much closer to the type of personality characteristics that help to build powerful brands. As we shall see below, brand personality adds a human touch to the cold and often impersonal world of technology.

The brand as a person

In Chapter 2 we talked about brand personality, and how successful consumer brands have used this aspect of brand building to attract and retain consumers. This dimension is particularly important to technology branding because it adds warmth and human touch to otherwise cold and impersonal products. The aim of developing a brand personality is to take the focus away from metal, wires, circuits, and other product components and features, and move toward the kind of relationship companies want to establish with the consumer. For example, Rolls-Royce's advertisement in Asia talks about strength, power and commitment, the hallmarks of a great champion, and the qualities that the company brings to Asia and its people. The words themselves are powerful and attractive in their own right. They are personality characteristics presented to the target audience in headlines that immediately capture attention, and that sum up the brand strengths of the company.

Another way to look at the issue of the brand as a person is to realize that the human brain has two hemispheres—one on the left, another on the right. Because they function differently, it is important for a brand to appeal to both sides. This means combining the rational dimension with the emotional component in your brand proposition.

Technology brands appeal very much to the rational side of people's minds through product features, gadgets, and the like, which some companies believe distinguish their products from others. In this age of parity, it is all too easy for competitors to copy those features and even improve on them. However, to achieve a sustainable competitive advantage, companies must capture the hearts and minds of consumers as well. Only then can they stand a chance of being perceived as truly different. If they build a brand personality for a product that has both an emotional and a rational appeal, then they are simulating the mind of the consumer, making their brand so much more attractive. This is explained in greater detail below.

Capturing consumers' hearts and minds

The structure of the human brain, with its left and right sides, has not escaped the attention of brand experts either. We can generalize by saying that one half of our brain—the left side—is concerned with logic and numbers, employing rational thinking and behavior. The other half—the right hemisphere—is concerned with emotion, dreams, creativity, and similar ways of thinking and doing things. Both sets of functions—one rational in nature, the other emotional—are important to people. It therefore makes sense to appeal to consumers by communicating with them in one of two ways, or better yet, in both ways if you want to appeal to both sides of their brains.

Branding recognizes the dual-brain capability and operates accordingly. Experts explain this by saying, quite rightly, that they appeal to the "head," or the left brain, and the "heart," or the right brain. This way of looking at the consumer started with packaged consumer goods, but has been adopted rapidly by practically every type of business in various industries. A good example of a fast-moving consumer goods company that uses large doses of emotion to sell its products is Häagen-Dazs. Romance and sensuality are the twin pillars of the Häagen-Dazs brand, making up the brand character to which the company steadfastly adheres in its product development and promotion. From its ice-cream cakes called "Truly Deeply, Madly" and "Heart of Hearts," to its advertisements and brochures depicting a young couple with their mouths around the same spoonful of ice cream, and the tagline "Dedicated to pleasure," the brand values are conveyed most consistently and effectively.

Using the Yin *and* Yang *model*

When you are building a brand for a technology company or product, it is important to give it a well-balanced personality, one that appeals to the rational and emotional sides of every consumer's minds. The best way to build a technology brand is to use the *Yin* and *Yang* model, as illustrated in Figure 3.

RATIONAL   EMOTIONAL

Figure 3: The *Yin* and *Yang* model of technology brand building

This model originates in Asian culture, where the *Yin* and *Yang* are complementary sides of every person and situation, needing balance to

establish order and harmony. Applied to branding, it emphasizes that
brand success also depends on its appeal to two sides—the rational and
the emotional—and that the two must work in harmony. If the *Yin*
represents the rational side (as exemplified by such brand attributes as
quality and reliability), then the brand must seek the *Yang* (representing
emotional attributes like a caring attitude and sophistication). The *Yin*
and *Yang* model, if applied to technology brands, brings that essential
harmony to the minds of buyers of technology products. Often
bewildered by the rational, nay, technical features and attributes of the
brand, they long for a balance of simplicity, peace of mind, and similar
attributes that will satisfy the emotional deprivation associated with
technology. As is often the case in real life, a well-balanced personality
is not only sensible, it is also likeable. And, like a person who can draw
upon different elements of his personality for different occasions, the *Yin*
and *Yang* approach to branding can be flexed to appeal to the rational
and emotional components of brand communications. An admirable
example of this approach is TAG Heuer.

TAG Heuer is a brand that works hard on the *Yin* and *Yang*
approach. Positioned as not just a brand of sports watches and
chronographs but as a prestigious fashion accessory, the brand is much
sought-after by sports enthusiasts, collectors, as well as the rich and
famous. The brand values of TAG Heuer have two sides that lend the
brand balance and harmony. On the rational side, the corresponding
attributes portrayed appear to be:

- sturdy
- robust
- versatile
- durable
- resilient
- technological savvy

As a technology product concerned with accuracy of the highest
degree, the brand must project the rational side of its character,
emphasizing the attributes necessary for a product to succeed. TAG
Heuer's sponsorship of Formula One racing reinforces the image it wants

to project by conveying the message that a superb technical capability is needed to time the world's fastest racing cars to thousandths of a second.

TAG Heuer also recognizes that emotion sells. As such, the personality characteristics it seems to project are the following:

- precise
- dashing
- challenging
- dynamic
- risky
- tough
- heroic

Reinforced by top athlete endorsements and truly powerful advertising that bring the emotional side of the brand to life, TAG Heuer has become a world-class brand, displacing or overtaking Rolex and other famous brands in the 20- to 40-year-old age group. For technology companies and products, the integration of emotional appeal in branding is critical to brand success. A watch is a watch is a watch—but TAG Heuer is a famous brand.

Using emotion to create trust and differentiation

The appeal to emotion is especially important to technology companies, not just for the reasons given above but also for reasons that have to do with the need to establish trust and differentiation in the minds of consumers. Companies can allay the almost pathological fear of technology that many people have by introducing a friendly and straightforward brand personality. Creating this personality requires an appeal to emotion, which provides consumers with a point of reference that distinguishes one brand from another, or one that establishes trust and differentiation.

As we pointed out above, there is so much rationality built into technology products that successful companies like Nokia concentrate heavily on the emotional appeal of their branding. (See the Nokia case study at the end of this chapter.) Apple Computers has also succeeded in appealing to the emotional side of its buyers' minds, with its futuristic and colorful iMAC. Steve Jobs, who obviously understands his consumers, says it is not so much essential to talk to them in gigabyte and terabyte terms as to give them something nice to look at, touch, and express themselves with.

Turning the rational into the emotional

Giving technology products an emotional appeal can be difficult, as their features can easily dominate marketing thinking. One way to turn rational attributes into emotional attractions is to think like consumers. For example, if the rational attribute or technical feature is speed, then you get to the emotional attribute by completing the phrase "which means that . . ." Here is an example:

- Brand X is faster than Y, which means that
- you can complete a task quicker than before/achieve more each day/will not be so stressed/enjoy better health and relax more, which means that
- you will have more time to spend on other important goals/with your family and friends/have a happier home life, which means that
- you will be more effective in your job/get better performance ratings/enjoy greater success.

Using this technique can often provide multiple opportunities for integrating emotional attraction into positioning, advertising, and promotion. The thinking process can apply to all the typical features and attributes of technology products and companies that a brand may possess, such as:

- reliability
- efficiency
- effectiveness
- cleanliness
- flexibility
- quality
- quietness

- durability
- toughness
- precision

What you are actually doing when you use this approach is identifying the key benefits associated with the product feature. People often do not really want products for the sake of having them; they want them for the benefits they will derive from them. This is particularly true of technology products. Companies must think like a consumer because the benefits carry emotional associations in people's minds. If only more product designers would think this way, they would likely produce products that mean more to consumers than ones that look good but do not mean much to buyers, having been designed according to what the designers wanted.

This process, which can actually be turned into a fun exercise with staff and colleagues, can yield outputs that do not just anticipate consumer thinking but are also useful for marketing communications and the formation of key messages for different customer groups.

Determining the tone and manner of advertising

In capturing the hearts and minds of their consumers, some technology companies use emotionally charged words and pictures in their advertisements. An example from the Internet company eToys.com is an advertisement released through the traditional, specifically print, media. It packs an emotional component into the benefits of visiting its site. Alongside a photograph of a child searching underwater for a starfish is copy that reads:

"You search by age,
interest or brand.
You browse through colorful
pages full of helpful hints.
You move from all kinds of toys to music,
books and videos at the click of a mouse.
You find the perfect gift for your child.

You choose a wrapping paper.
You add a card.
You get a hug."

While the photograph could initially lead others to believe that eToys.com does sell living things, the advertisement nevertheless succeeds in getting parents to think about their children in an emotional way.

The point we want to make here is that the tone and manner of advertising must reflect the personality of the brand. The words must be the type of words that the brand "person" would use; the commercial talent or advertisement model should effectively project the brand personality and its target audience; background shots should be appropriate to the brand character. For example, in one Mercedes-Benz commercial, the opening shot is of Tiffany's flagship store, the talent looks successful, well-dressed, sophisticated, and the background shots are of glamorous locations and celebration events. All this adds up to a proper representation of the Mercedes brand's charismatic personality.

The brand as a symbol

Brands are more than logos and trademarks. This book should demonstrate that fact more than anything else. But some brands are so popular that just a fleeting glimpse of their logos will trigger off certain thoughts and feelings in people's minds. Mercedes-Benz is a classic example of this. Its logo, consisting of a three-pointed star enclosed in a circle, represents a host of attributes such as prestige, status, high-quality engineering, and motoring precision. Nike's swoosh sign also has powerful associations. Technology company and product brands may not be enjoying this kind of brand recognition yet, but it may not be far-fetched to imagine that those that are working hard to gain powerful associations by using ubiquitous signs—for instance, "Intel Inside"—may well be on their way to realizing their dream.

Historically, one would think of Intel as anything but a marketing-driven organization. Today, however, Intel's brand recognition is among the best in all sectors of industry. What makes this achievement most impressive is that Intel is a business-to-business brand, and sells products that are invisible to the end user.

Compared to the PC market of the 1980s and early 1990s, the coming years do not look so bright for providers of PC technology. The commercial sector is evolving rapidly toward a replacement market, and the consumer market represents a real challenge to vendors' net profits. Consolidation among PC manufacturers, intense price competition, and profit margin pressure have further contributed to overall vendor anxiety. These factors affect Intel, the supplier of the most expensive PC component.

The development of the "Intel Inside" campaign represented the first stage of the transformation. The familiar Intel logos on PC packaging and bezels gave Intel visibility among end users and established trust with the consumer. While some original equipment manufacturers (OEMs) turned cold to the campaign, arguing that it reduced the value of the OEM name, Intel carried it on with TV, radio, and print advertising.

Intel is now executing the next major phase of the transformation. Besides an even more visible marketing, the company has launched sub-brands targeted at distinct markets and users. This approach is in stark contrast to Intel's historical "one size eventually fits all" approach. This is where a state-of-the-art processor would be introduced at the high end (i.e., for servers and workstations), initially at very high prices which will then be scaled down across the price bands of mainstream commercial desktops and, eventually, of mobile, embedded, and low-cost consumer systems.

Various sub-brands make up Intel's product portfolio, including Xeon, Pentium, and Celeron. Each sub-brand is differentiated through packaging, cache implementations, and bus designs, with more permutations intended for the future. To optimize price and performance in each brand segment, Intel has added commensurate complexity to its core logic portfolio and road map.

When a company reaches the stage where the icon that represents its brand has gained global recognition, there is little need to talk about the products themselves, because people are buying the brand and all that it stands for. Intel has achieved global brand status, and is now among the top five most valuable brands in the world.

The brand as a product

Any successful brand manager will tell you that a brand is not an excuse for a poor product or service. Indeed, it is absolutely essential that any brand is at least as good as competitor brands in terms of quality. We noted this earlier in the chapter when we looked at some data on quality and customer service, and how it can impact on company performance. This is why Nestlé and other manufacturers sample millions of units of each of their brands every year. With technology products, quality assurance is every bit as critical to the consumer in making brand choices. As Ford said, "Quality Is Job Number One."

Poor quality is always bound to affect sales, such as what happened to the Jaguar brand. Its sales went down some years ago because of inconsistent product quality. In contrast, Motorola enjoys brand success, thanks to its six-sigma quality model. Sony, too, constantly strives for the highest quality standards. In the world of technology, there is just no substitute for a good product. You cannot escape from having a high-quality product or service when the goal is to build a strong brand.

In addition to the continual search for quality, another facet of the brand as a product, especially in technology, is the need to keep the product relevant to the audience you are targeting, and to the position you seek to occupy in their minds. This means relentlessly researching the needs and wants of your customer base, and tirelessly refreshing the brand in terms, for instance, of product features and attributes while maintaining your message. Indeed, one of the most critical issues for technology companies is keeping up with change in a relevant and consistent way. Customers will buy what they need and want, not necessarily what a company thinks they should. The Nokia case study at the end of this chapter gives a good example of the importance attached to remembering that the brand is a product.

Quality is important even in the world of e-commerce. Service recovery cannot do without it. Mistakes are bound to happen in the virtual sales world. Amazon.com has demonstrated what it takes to provide legendary service when things go wrong.

The brand as a position

Technology companies must work hard on positioning because they have to distinguish themselves from the crowd. A brand will not succeed unless it secures a specific position in consumers' minds. As positioning is based on perceptions, managing perceptions is the basis of good brand management. A strong position is a function of a strong message that tells consumers why a certain brand is better than competing brands. IBM has been consistently positioning itself as a business solution provider for the last three years, using the tag line "Solutions for a small planet" and an integrated communications campaign plus staff training to back up the position. (Chapter 4 discusses positioning in detail.)

The brand as a culture

Finally, in the most successful companies—or those that have built really powerful brands—we see that everyone in the organization moves behind the brand, is motivated by it, wants it to succeed, and will do anything to keep that brand in its leadership position. The brand is a source of pride, of belonging, of esteem, with everyone thinking about it every day at work. If you think this is fantasy, visit companies like the Disney Corporation and observe how employees get a lift at the mere thought of working for a famous brand.

Needless to say, the creation of a strong brand culture does not happen by chance. A great deal of training and development work goes into making it happen. Intel, for example, has extensive training programs to help staff understand and apply its brand values. Its core values are:

- risk taking
- quality
- discipline
- customer-orientation

- results-orientation
- "great place to work" mindset

Intel goes the extra mile to help its employees live the brand. While not all of its core values are brand personality attributes (and arguably, more personality-type characteristics could have given Intel a more human face), the training is there to create the desired corporate culture. For instance, Intel looked at role models in its organization for the brand value of risk taking. After analyzing the employees' behavior based on this characteristic, Intel created a suitable training program with training kits for individuals and teams. The value was, of course, clearly defined in terms of the employees' ability to:

- embrace change
- challenge the status quo
- listen to all ideas and viewpoints
- encourage and reward informed risk taking
- learn from one's successes and mistakes

The risk taking kit provided included ten items such as group and individual exercises and resource lists. It also included specific advice on potential problems, such as how to balance risk taking with another value—say, quality. Intel also produced video interviews with the role models. This served as a good motivation not only for the role models themselves but also for other staff who realized that they could be good risk takers too. Intel dealt with the other values in a similar fashion. The outcome was a 360-degree core management survey with global coverage.

Other companies are also well known for taking brand into performance management. GE, for example, links employee performance on brand values with overall remuneration via the performance appraisal system. Companies with powerful brands have built them by realizing that the brand is everything, and that everyone must play his part in making the brand values come to life.

For technology brands, the fear inherent in people looking to buy hi-tech products means that extra attention has to be given to delivering on the brand promise. Whether this is by warranty, service quality, after-sales care, or a combination of any the elements that can affect customer experience, a company must make every effort to exceed expectations. Such a resolve is even more critical to service brands. As we shall see in Chapter 6, which is about Internet branding, competitors are only a click of a mouse away if each brand experience fails to impress a customer.

Brand extension

Brand extension is one of the main aspirations of many brand owners and managers. Extending the brand to related, and even non-related, products and services can mean big profits. This is why Coca-Cola has moved into clothing, and why Richard Branson recently declared that his company, Virgin Group, was aiming to become a global Internet brand. The idea for Virgin is to bring together all of its products and services (from planes and trains, to cola, clothing and cosmetics, to mobile phones and music stores, to financial services products and radio) into one big sales site. However, Virgin is not falling into the trap of just selling its own products. It wants to become an e-commerce portal like Amazon.com.

Branson said, "If British Airways is selling better products than Virgin Atlantic, we'll sell the British Airways product." He added, "If Fidelity is offering a better financial product than Virgin Direct, we'll recommend the Fidelity product." He is not worried about the Web site cannibalizing offline brands, saying that it is a fact of life that "the Internet will kill off some of our businesses and severely damage a lot of conventional industry."

Time will tell whether the company and its Internet site, www.virgin.com, will be successful—it is not even in the top ten most visited sites in Britain yet. But Branson cannot be underestimated. "If we could be worth just half of AOL, I'd be happy," he said. The entrepreneurial talent that has characterized his business drive and achievements may well be enough to get him where he wants his company to be. The Virgin site is certainly worth looking at, as it promises a user-friendly experience for its visitors, coupled with the fun and youthful attributes of the Virgin brand personality.

To extend a brand, a company must ensure that the parent brand has a strong image. But even if this requirement is met, brands can only be stretched so far. Corporate brands can go further than product brands, but they have limits too. Virgin was largely unsuccessful in its cosmetics and vodka forays, for example. The suitability of a brand for extension depends entirely on whether the consumer will accept it or not. Fastidious research is best done before any risk is taken. Nike Inc., for example, has had its ups and downs with brand extensions, but with its entry into the hi-tech world, it would appear to have a winner. Nike is going digital, inspired by the success of its beautifully designed running watch range. The company has had some mediocre performances with previous brand extensions, such as its casual apparel and some sports equipment lines, but the new extensions are much closer to the core Nike sports passion brand values. Unveiled in May 2000 were sports and electronics product, such as a portable heart-rate monitor, a hi-tech walkie-talkie radio, a digital audio player, and a wrist compass. Also planned are a watch that measures the speed and distance covered by runners, and accessories for the products. Nike is so committed to the hi-tech future that it has set up a completely new division called Techlab. The aim of this business unit is to develop sports technology products by creating alliances with top technology companies like S3 Inc., a maker of Rio products that play MP3 files, which will produce the Nike digital audio player. The familiar Nike trademark swoosh sign will provide all the emotional associations for consumers, and the products will have vibrant colors such as "fire warm," "green leaf," and "cool sparkle."

Brand guardianship

Creating a brand is one thing; keeping it fresh and well maintained is another. From a product point of view, this is not really a problem to hi-tech companies, which tend to have big research and development budgets as well as substantial new product development schedules. However, from a brand perspective, it is all too easy to concentrate on product innovation and ignore the brand and its image. Companies must constantly look after and improve upon all areas of the brand promise, whether they are communications, service quality, or the customer experience of its totality. And while making sure that such improvements are made to the brand proposition, they must maintain brand consistency and appropriateness at the same time, both of which are vital to the development of consumer trust.

Making technology mean something

Technology is only as good as its use, and companies that are technology-based have to focus their brand building on making technology mean something to the consumer. Several hi-tech companies are currently trying to do this, but few have successfully made an impact on consumer thinking. The two case studies below represent good examples of how a great deal of thought and work has made technology mean something to people's lives.

CASE STUDY 1
NOKIA
Building a powerful technology brand

The world of parity has hit the mobile phone market just as it has many other technology product categories. The products range from the simple to the complex, but every manufacturer has, of course, the latest features in his products. Leapfrogging in sales between brands frequently occurs based on design. But overall the market is predictable, with Nokia, Motorola, and Ericsson fighting it out at the top, and several less successful brands like Samsung, Philips, Siemens, and Panasonic trying hard to make inroads into their top competitors' market share. So what makes the difference between the most successful and less successful brands? It certainly is not what product features are offered. How, then, do consumers choose? The answer seems to be what the brand names mean to them.

Nokia Group, the Finland-based manufacturer of mobile phones, has been steadily working on its corporate brand name and the management of consumer perceptions over the last few years. Its efforts have paid off, because it is now the number one brand in many markets around the world, effectively dislodging Motorola from that position. The brand has been built using the principles described above, and has been consistently well managed across all markets. Nokia has succeeded in lending personality to its products, without even giving them names. In other words, it has not created any sub-brands but has concentrated on the corporate brand, giving individual products a generic brand personality. Only numeric descriptors are used for the products, which do not even appear on the products themselves. Such is the strength of the corporate brand.

Nokia has succeeded where other big brand names have so far failed, chiefly by putting across the human face of technology—taking and dominating the emotional high ground. It has done so in the following way.

Nokia brand personality

Nokia has detailed many personality characteristics for its brand, but employees do not have to remember every characteristic. They do, however, have to remember the overall impression of the list of attributes, as you would when thinking about someone you have met. As the focus is on customer relationships, the Nokia personality is like a trusted friend. Building friendship and trust is at the heart of the Nokia brand. And the human dimension created by the brand personality carries over into the positioning strategy for the brand.

Nokia positioning

When Nokia positions its brand in the crowded mobile phone marketplace, its message must clearly bring together the technology and human side of its offer in a powerful way. The specific message that is conveyed to consumers in every advertisement and market communication (though not necessarily in these words) is *"Only Nokia Human Technology enables you to get more out of life."*

In many cases, this is represented by the tag line, "We call this *human technology.*"™ This gives consumers a sense of trust and consideration by the company, as though to say that Nokia understands what they want in life, and how it can help. And it knows that technology is really only an enabler so that you—the customer—can enjoy a better life. Nokia thus uses a combination of aspirational, benefit-based, emotional features, and competition-driven positioning strategies. It owns the "human" dimension of mobile communications, leaving its competitors wondering what to own (or how to position themselves), having taken the best position for itself.

Nokia product design

Nokia is a great brand because it knows that the essence of the brand needs to be reflected in everything the company does, especially those that impact on the consumer. Product design is clearly critical to the success of the brand, but how does Nokia manage to inject personality into product design? The answer is that it gives a great deal of thought to how the user of its phones will experience the brand, and how it can make that experience reflect its brand character. The large display screen, for example, is the "face" of the phone. Nokia designers describe it as "the eye into the soul of the product." The shape of the phones is curvy and easy to hold. The faceplates and their different colors can be changed to fit the personality, lifestyle, and mood of the user. The soft key touch pads also add to the feeling of friendliness, expressing the brand personality. Product design focuses on the consumer and his needs, and is summed up in the slogan, "human technology."

Nokia now accounts for over half of the value of the Finland stock market, and has taken huge market shares from its competitors. According to one brand valuation study carried out in mid-1999, it ranked 11th on the world's most valuable brand list, making it the highest-ranking non-U.S. brand. As has been pointed out, it has unseated Motorola. Nokia achieved its brilliant feat through consistent branding, backed by first-class logistics and manufacturing, all of which revolve around what consumers want.

Summary

The greater the influence that technology has on a company's product and service range, the more it needs to market them in an emotional way. A rational appeal has to be balanced with an emotional one—a critical issue in brand building. Technology companies can best do this by building strong brand personalities. Brand personalities are particularly important in building the corporate brand, because these are where consumers look to find the trust and confidence they desperately seek in technology products and companies. Young technology companies should create their corporate brand personality as early as possible so that they can gain a reputation for understanding the rational and emotional needs of consumers.

Brand builder's checklist

1. What are the features/attributes of your brand (company, product, service)?
2. What are the practical benefits associated with each of these features/attributes?
3. Can you extend these features and benefits to form emotional associations for the consumer?
4. What are the emotional reasons why customers might buy your products/services?
5. What values does your company subscribe to?
6. What are the rational and emotional personality characteristics of your brand?
7. What can you do to bring these personality characteristics to life?
8. How can you use the brand personality to attract and retain more customers?
9. How can you best deliver on the promise of your brand personality?
10. How are you going to generate more trust in the brand–customer relationship?

CASE STUDY 2
PHILIPS
Strengthening a global brand

Philips is a hi-tech global company with a traditionally low profile. Until recently, if you asked anyone if he knew the Philips brand name, the likelihood was that he would say yes. However, he might not have known what Philips provides in the way of its total product range, and might have associated the brand name and company with traditional technology. The "Let's Make Things Better" global brand campaign has raised the Philips profile, and provided it with a more focused and distinctive personality.

Royal Philips Electronics—its proper name—is a giant company. Established in 1891 as a lamp factory, it now has over 100 different businesses, over 200 production sites, and carries out research and development in more than 40 countries. Its sales and service outlets cover 150 countries, and it has a total workforce upwards of 230,000 employees. It has a strong technology base, spending over 5% of sales on research and development, and owning some 10,000 patents. Its portfolio covers a wide variety of product categories, including:

- semiconductors
- TV
- video
- audio
- PC peripherals
- digital networks
- lighting
- medical systems
- mobile phones
- domestic appliances
- personal care products

The "Let's Make Things Better" campaign is still part of a global corporate branding initiative aimed at motivating both consumers and employees. It was, to use Intel's own words, a brand "renaissance."

The company's slogan is all about emphasizing what technology, Philips products in particular, can do for people—it is essentially about the benefits they can bring to people and the world in general. A keystone of the campaign was the premise that, if you can convince people that you can help improve their lives, they will more likely believe that you can help improve the world. The campaign thus had to appear credible, real, and experiential. It had to be human as opposed to philosophical and philanthropic, and not just another typical corporate overclaim.

Brand personality and "star products"

To humanize the positioning that the company wanted, and to base it on reality, use was made of the Philips brand personality and "star products." The brand personality consisted of three characteristics:

a) human

b) imaginative

c) seductive

This personality summed up the "Philips Tribe"—the people that represented the aspirational face of Philips, had a distinctive attitude and style, and were very comfortable with technology.

Aimed at the consumer as the center of the company's actions, "Star products" with "star features technologies" were used to support the brand promise of "better." "Let's Make Things Better" was not to be merely an advertising tag line but a way of working with the consumer, to build consistency in brand communications and product development, and make Philips unique.

Consumer target groups

Prior to the development of the campaign, the company had carried out a global consumer segmentation study that included 14,000 interviews in 17 countries, where questions about consumer satisfaction and new product development were asked. Five target segments were identified, namely:

1. *Technology-enabled*:
   People who use technology to solve problems and get things done.
2. *Technology-status*:
   People who use technology as a badge.
3. *Dream seekers*:
   People who aspire to a better life for themselves through technology.
4. *Family first*:
   People who seek a better life for their family through technology.
5. *Amuse me*:
   People who use technology for amusement and as a form of escapism.

The aim was to get consumers to think, "My life can be better with Philips."

The advertising challenge

The advertising challenge was to put Philips on consumers' pre-decided consideration list without presenting Philips technology as too simple (like yesterday's technology) or too complex (too challenging and alienating). The final message cut across three dimensions:

1. *Technology*: "Wow! It can do that."
2. *Self*: "Wow! I can do that."
3. *Life*: "Wow! Things can get better."

The tone and manner of the advertisements should not only represent the brand personality; it should also bring these three dimensions together with a sense of wonder and in a youthful, experiential way. In the resulting commercial, the "Getting Better" element of the advertising execution used the Beatles' classic song, with the line "I've got to admit it's getting better, it's getting better all the time."

A truly global campaign

The Philips commercial is a true global campaign, having been produced in some of the leading creative centers around the world, including New York, Hong Kong, Singapore, and Mumbai. The global launch was done simultaneously in August 1998. Because of the campaign's extensive global consumer insight, it was possible to create advertising which had cross-local and regional relevance. This went a long way toward helping Philips achieve its strategic brand objective of showing "one face to the market." This campaign is still running today, and its impact on delivering the brand promise in a persuasive manner to consumers globally is being tracked on a monthly basis. Compared to pre-campaign benchmarks, the brand has shown improvement in practically all areas that can impact on brand strength, including brand preference, top-of-mind awareness, and ratings on specific image indicators and attributes.

Philips global brand management

Philips has developed a global brand management system to manage, develop, and guard its brand. There are two missions for the global brand management, namely:

1. *Internal:*
    * To serve as a focal point for marketing, brand, and image management
    * To be the custodian of the Philips brand
    * To integrate the consumer into Philips
2. *External:*
    * To build Philips into a top-ranking, world-class consumer brand
    * To increase shareholder value
    * To put forward one Philips "face" to the market

The responsibilities of Philips' global brand management are to:

* advise product divisions on product positioning and new product introductions
* manage the Philips brand image worldwide
* develop Philips' marketing processes, practices, and procedures to a world-class standard
* "own" the relationship with the advertising agency

- ensure proper use and application of research data (image and product)
- work with product divisions to hire and develop world-class marketing talent
- stimulate the quality of innovation of marketing thinking
- give marketing guidance and support to businesses

This comprehensive brand management system includes units such as

- global consumer and market intelligence
- marketing competence center
- regional brand champions

Of particular note are the five regional brand champions, whose primary responsibilities are to:

- provide cross-product division synergies
- increase consumer focus
- bring the Philips Consumer Electronics strategy to life
- bring one Philips "face" to the market
- formulate strategic brand marketing plans
- upgrade marketing talent with the region/businesses

The structure of Philips' global brand management is still undergoing some evolution, but the intent and mission of this rather unique entity within Philips remains unchanged.

There are many more aspects to Philips' brand management. Suffice to say, however, that it is one of the best global examples of how to manage and develop a technology brand.

4

Positioning Strategies of Technology Companies and Products

An important part of the process of building any strong brand is differentiation—that is, the creation of one or more differences that may be tangible or intangible for a company or product. Indeed, this is the purpose of branding—to create an identity that is different from all those offered by competitors. In the cluttered marketplace, if you do not stand out from the crowd, you are dead.

Creating a unique identity through positioning

Positioning ensures that your company, products, and services are not seen as commodities but as unique identities. Differentiation occurs in the minds of consumers, not in the minds of marketers. Positioning, on the other hand, refers to the strategies a company employs to ensure that the key differences occupy a unique position in people's minds. The questions that positioning seeks to answer are therefore those that are uppermost in the minds of people who are considering buying a particular product or service from a choice of companies, namely:

- Why is it different?
- Why is it better?

These questions largely determine whether the consumer buys a particular brand or not. They are particularly relevant to technology brands, as opposed to traditional fast-moving consumer product brands, because people do not normally buy on impulse when it comes to technology brands. The fact that differentiation exists in people's minds makes it clear that consumer perception counts, which power brands manage well. Perception can be fact or fiction. But to consumers it does not matter, because to them, perception is reality. So positioning is all about gaining a share of the consumer mind rather than a share of the market. It is all about standing out from the crowd.

Positioning at its most basic level involves establishing a favorable opinion or image in people's minds, because if we have a good reputation or image, we are standing out from the competition. But many companies are too preoccupied with measuring and managing image instead of projecting and delivering the brand promise in every possible way to create the desired image. Those that constantly research consumer perception of their image—usually through customer satisfaction surveys—are often disappointed with the findings. They often try to rectify matters by improving customer service rather than looking at whether the brand promise is the right one for their target customers, or identifying what those customers really expect from the brand.

Managing the brand by positioning techniques and actions that project what the brand stands for is the best way to manage image. Many companies fail to realize that they can influence people's perceptions (image) through the skillful deployment of positioning strategies, and so influence their destiny in a proactive, as opposed to a reactive, way. For this reason, some say a brand is really only a position; that the position makes the brand as it creates value in the minds of the target audience. Setting these claims aside, we can say without any doubt at all that establishing a strong position is critical to the development of a powerful brand.

The positioning problem for technology brands

As we have stated, consumers do not buy technology products on impulse. They have to be convinced about the performance and the brand itself. And as we have seen in Chapter 3, trust is vital to technology purchases, considering the ease with which technology products can be replicated, resulting in a marketplace full of branded products with similar features.

Differentiation is essential; so is positioning a brand to break away from the pack in people's minds. Not only does a technology brand have to be seen as different; it must be perceived as being better, too, so that it can be credible in the marketplace.

Failure to employ positioning strategies that establish trust in a brand and help it to break away from the parity problem will mean that the product will only achieve commodity status, and thus will never be a powerful brand. What, then, are the options in terms of positioning strategies that technology companies might employ?

Positioning strategies

There are many different positioning strategies that can be effective for companies. (See *Strategic Positioning*, Oxford University Press, 1999, for a comprehensive look at positioning.) The most important of these for technology companies, products, and services are as follows:

- problem–solution
- simplicity and ease
- features and benefits
- emotional appeal
- aspirational appeal
- personality
- being number one
- innovation
- value added

Problem–solution

> *"I have no love of technology for technology's sake… Only solutions for customers."*
>
> Cisco CEO John Chambers

As technology is a vast enabler, it often enables consumers to solve specific problems. With the exception of people who love to learn about technical things, most people do not understand technology but nonetheless look for, and appreciate, what it can do to help them.

The principle of problem–solving is powerful. Practically every person in the world would like assistance in solving problems. As life gets more stressful, and the pressure for results more acute, problems seem to mount up at work and in the home.

Many hi-tech companies are now adopting a positioning stance based on the appeal of solving consumer problems. One of the pioneers of this strategy was IBM, which realized in the early 1990s that its multi-billion-dollar losses were, in no small measure, due to its lack of understanding of what consumers really wanted. By ceasing to concentrate on developing and selling the products it thought the market wanted, and instead packaging solutions to solve the problems of its customers, it made a giant step forward in both thinking and profitability. Its tag line, "Solutions for a Small Planet," summed up this new approach, and encapsulated its new market philosophy and desired position. IBM partly delivered on its promise by recruiting and training several thousand employees to act as consultants to clients in problem diagnosis and problem-solving.

Motorola's product Digital DNA™ is described in advertisements as belonging to Motorola Embedded Solutions, capitalizing on the problem–solution positioning strategy. NEC carries the "NEC Multimedia Solutions" headline in its advertisements. One piece of copy reads: "Whatever the size and type of your business, you'll need multimedia solutions to keep it going." Fujitsu says, "We deliver an unsurpassed array of Internet solutions, from infrastructure to electronic commerce. Our IT solutions, from global servers to application software, are powering the new Internet economy."

A print advertisement from NTT Communications is another interesting example. Leaving nothing to the imagination, the ad carries two large pictures, one of which shows off a heap of apparently old, broken, or unused string instruments such as violins, and has the caption, "Harder Problems? Welcome." The copy partly reads, "Go ahead. Tell us your problems. Your hardest problems. And we'll provide you with the solutions. Arcstar, NTT Communications' global solution brand, has the answers to all your telecommunications problems." The second picture has an orchestra playing all the instruments, ably conducted by a man with his back to the audience. The caption reads, "A trusted solution service from NTT Communications." A list of services follows. The main tag line accompanying the logo is, "Your Trusted Partner in Network Solutions." Although very much an "in your face" ad, it does put across the positioning very strongly. The pictures and tag line add a touch of emotion to what is otherwise a very rational business proposition.

For Internet companies trying to develop their brands, the problem–solution positioning strategy offers a great deal of opportunity. As convenience is one of the core consumer needs of Internet users, it makes sense to adopt such a positioning. Consider shopping—generally regarded by many as a chore these days. As such, online bookstores and grocery stores have generated a lot of interest. People do not want to spend a valuable part of their day driving to a shop or store, finding a parking space, struggling through hordes of other equally grumpy people, waiting in a queue to pay a disinterested assistant, and driving all the way back again. Companies like Streamline, an online grocery retailer in the United States, are building good positions because they are solving the problems of frustrated shoppers. Currently, less than 1% of U.S. households order groceries online. This number is projected to rise to between 10% and 15% of the groceries and household consumer goods market, worth over US$400 billion, by 2007. Solving people's problems can be a lucrative business! On the technical side, Getronic's (www.getronics.com) positioning is totally focused on being "a leading provider of e-generation ICT Solutions and Services."

In a world of bewildering choices, consumers are looking for solutions to their problems, and the high-flying Internet companies such as Yahoo and E*Trade have helped consumers cut through the clutter and reach their goals. EDS goes one step further than most, saying, "We help solve the unsolvable. Consistently from country to country. With flexibility. Reliability. And security." Its tag line is "solved." But can we really believe that brand promise?

There seems to be no end to the claims. The issue here is that positioning is aimed at differentiation, but this positioning strategy itself is becoming a commodity. In fact, we are getting to the stage where we see so many solutions, we might not have enough problems to go round! If you are going to use this strategy, then combine it with one or more of the others.

Simplicity and ease

Technology is complex, however you look at it. Still, some companies capitalize on this fact. Recognizing the worries and concerns of people about complex technologies, they offer simplicity and ease of use as their positioning strategy. Sometimes this is connected to the solutions positioning strategy, as in the case of Concert from AT&T and BT. Concert is a company created to "provide simpler solutions to the complexities of global communications." Its sign-off line in print ads reads, "Global communications simplified to the nth degree."

NTT Communications has also adopted this positioning strategy with Arcstar. It uses headlines in advertisements like "We make it simple" and copy such as "Make your business in Asia simple. With help from NTT Communications." Another example of a company that uses this positioning strategy is Cisco Systems. When talking about its Content Networking services, it says, "Through Cisco Content Networking, Internet business applications can be deployed simply and quickly."

Making things simple and easy in a complex world can be a powerful brand proposition.

Features and benefits

Basing a positioning on the communication of features and benefits is probably the most often used, and least effective, strategy for hi-tech companies, if used on its own. Focusing on the physical features or attributes of technology products alone does not differentiate one hi-tech product from another. The age of parity has squashed the effectiveness of telling people about features as a brand builder, although it is a necessary part of the communications mix to demonstrate to consumers that your product is state-of-the-art. When addressing segments of the market such as those who actively seek out new technology, it does become more important. Nevertheless, when other competitors have the same features in their products, additional strategies are needed to translate consumer interest into purchase.

Stressing the benefits associated with features is useful, as consumers sometimes do not see these immediately. A feature, for its own sake, is of little use until its benefit is explained. For example, if a particular technology product makes things easier for people to do something, it will be appreciated. This is a positioning that Microsoft uses. Canon has also embarked on this positioning strategy, with a commercial copy that gives an insight not just into the positioning but into the brand personality too, saying:

> "In a world full of words like 'digital,' 'technology,' and 'multimedia,' Canon keeps things bright, simple, and fun."

The sign-off reads, "Technology that makes you smile—Canon." The commercial, unfortunately, does not radiate fun and happiness.

Emotional appeal

The Canon example combines the appeal of simplicity with an appeal to emotion. Emotional appeal is one major area where technology companies are learning fast from consumer branding. The uses of emotion in branding technology and other products have been discussed in earlier chapters. Here, however, are interesting positioning examples. Sometimes, technology companies try to appeal to the hearts and minds of consumers by introducing emotional characteristics into their advertisements, by talking to their audience using emotional words and emotional pictures. In a Twinhead computer commercial, the question posed is, "What do you look for in a notebook?" The reply comes from the voices of talent representing various age groups, young and old alike, using words that also represent the brand character, namely:

- freedom
- excitement

- power
- innovation
- style

These are all emotionally charged words, and provide answers to the question that few people would argue with. To allay people's rational fear of technology, the last part of the commercial shows a young boy with his grandmother using a Twinhead notebook and saying the words "user-friendly." Twinhead signs itself off as "The Notebook Specialist," but not before supporting its brand statement with an Intel endorsement and the familiar, almost reassuring, musical notes of the Intel sign-off. Twinhead, which is not a global brand, clearly recognizes that it has to work hard on the trust element when it is competing in a category stocked with well-known brand names like Acer, Toshiba, and IBM. It does so by appealing directly and strongly to the rational and the emotional aspects of people's minds, and by co-branding with Intel.

Aspirational appeal

The world of branding recognizes the hopes and aspirations of every human being. Everyone hopes for a better life. The pursuit of prestige, success, status, luxury, power, and the natural tendency toward hero adulation are themes brands can use to tap into the psyche of consumers in a big way. With a cleverly thought-out brand positioning, companies can appeal to many market segments and multi-faceted sets of needs. Brands are expressions of these motivational drives, and allow people to demonstrate their success. Many luxury consumer brands such as Rolex, TAG Heuer, Mercedes-Benz, BMW, and Lexus have combined technology with aspirational appeals to top the charts. And in the info-communications and electronics field, Motorola's 1999 annual report declares that it is "committed to being the link between people's dreams and technology's promise." Meanwhile, the former somewhat boring business but now more exciting spin-off company of HP, Agilent Technologies, positions itself around the theme of "Dreams Made Real." (See the case study on Agilent at the end of this chapter.)

Personality

Building a brand personality for the company or product is a powerful addition to positioning strategy. (Chapters 2 and 3 explain how this is done.) Brand personality can be boosted tremendously by endorsements and sponsorships involving famous personalities or well-known talent.

Hi-tech companies are no different when it comes to using well-known personalities and celebrities to endorse their products and companies. Celebrities sell. Many marketers use "the cool factor," as this strategy is sometimes called, to stay on top. They persuade entertainment personalities not just to appear in commercials but to use their products publicly. Thus, companies provide many celebrity endorsers with their products in the hope that they will use them in public, and be photographed by the media while doing so.

TAG Heuer, for example, gave Elton John, a known watch collector, a special edition watch. The same company gives watches to prominent people at the Oscar awards night. Susan Nicholas, president of TAG Heuer (U.S.), said that the Hollywood stars are trendsetters. So if people see them wearing a particular brand of watch, they will readily consider it "cool" and may just decide to buy the same brand. TAG Heuer has also used sports personalities such as Boris Becker and Mikka Hakkinen for similar reasons.

Other companies have gone as far as setting up offices in Los Angeles with the sole aim of pursuing Hollywood stars. Motorola, for instance, opened up an office there and created a position called director of entertainment marketing. The incumbent, David Pinskey, said finding people in Hollywood who have the kind of image that Motorola wants— cool and cutting-edge—and getting them to use Motorola phones is well worth the effort, because "they become a walking commercial for us." Hence, Motorola regularly sends mobile phones to high-profile personalities. Among the celebrities that have been seen using its products are Tom Cruise and Mel Gibson. Similarly, Nikon has given samples of its latest models to Jamie Lee Curtis and Steven Spielberg.

Both Motorola and Nikon have also made it to the Oscars. Motorola once instructed its staff to stand at the side of the stage and give the winners samples of their product, thinking they just might use them to call their loved ones immediately with the great news, and all the while be seen on camera—a ploy that worked with celebrities like Nicolas Cage and Susan Sarandon, both former Oscar winners. Nikon's compact camera also got into the show, with Tom Hanks being one of the stars shown using it, much to the company's delight, of course. According to the general manager of Consumer Marketing, Nancy Carr, "No amount of advertising in the world could equal the coverage we get from donating to the Oscars." Nikon puts it thus: the Oscar event is "the perfect venue to build brand awareness."

Both Motorola and Nikon take the game one step further by getting their products into certain movies—a strategy described by Motorola's Pinskey as "intensive product placement." They even hire agents to find new scripts where Motorola products might have some use. What's more, they pay film producers for, say, at least four seconds of exposure for their products. Motorola phones have been shown in films like *Wag the Dog*, *As Good As It Gets*, and *The General's Daughter*. Nikon had the same opportunity in *The Lost World*.

Being number one

Being number one—or first mover advantage, as it is sometimes called—generates perceptions of leadership. In the hi-tech field it can work wonders for the brand and create an image of being different, even if product service and quality may be the same as those of the other major players. This is essentially what has happened to Amazon.com, which remains the brand leader in its field, even though other companies offer similar products and services. Brands such as Amazon and Onsale have benefited greatly by being the first in their category to go to the Net. Being first can result in lasting and dominant market share, even when competition comes in.

The number one position is also very important for software companies. Being on top affords one the opportunity to get a large network of users. This in itself makes the company's product more attractive for compatibility reasons. Research shows that once people have invested their time in learning how to use a particular software product, they are reluctant to switch to another brand. In the service industry, it is also relevant. Andersen Consulting was the first company to position itself as a technology consulting specialist. Now the other consulting companies are following, and this is what is important for the consulting firm brand—to be perceived as the leader in its field. If you are embarking on this positioning strategy for your business, however, remember that if you cannot remain on top, or at least give a semblance of being number one, the perception gap could damage your image.

Some try to claim being on top retrospectively, which is Sun Microsystems' response to the Internet gold rush, using the tag line, "We're the dot in .com." The company claims authenticity and pioneer status by asserting in advertisements that it has been taking companies into the Network Age for the better part of 16 years, "from ISPs like UUNET and Earthlink to entertainment companies like Sony. From e-commerce businesses like Music Boulevard to portals like Excite." Better late than never, and smacking a little of desperation, it does become harder to convince people about your number one status on a historical basis. But Sun does have some good commercials to make the point.

Such an approach is in stark contrast to Oracle's strategy, whose supporting line of "software powers the Internet" is backed by a claim that "65 of the top 100 Fortune 500 companies run Oracle for e-business." Informix also quotes statistics to bolster its "number one" positioning strategy by saying, "Pick up a phone anywhere in the world and there's an eight in ten chance you're connected, thanks to Informix software. Shop at nine of the world's top ten retailers and 18 of the world's 20 largest supermarkets, and Informix completes your sale." Informix's tag line is "Way to Web."

Innovation

Being number one in your field depends on innovation to a large degree, but being regarded as the pioneer in the hi-tech field is harder to maintain. Others, however, have managed to attain this position and keep at it, such as Dell and Apple. Steve Jobs, for instance, often refers to innovation as part of Apple's strategic competitive advantage, with statements like "We have so much innovation while the rest of the PC industry is in a coma—with brains switched off." Apple backs up these claims, of course, with souped-up iBooks, the introduction of the world's first-ever personal computer, and a promise to make a computer "so beautiful, you want to lick it."

Another example is Siemens, which has joined the mobile communications battle, and sums up its services thus: "Innovating the mobile world." Others find so many technological breakthroughs taking place all the time that it is tough to be involved in all of them. Having focus is not enough. Innovation needs massive research and development commitment, not to mention state-of-the-art knowledge. Some companies invest heavily in research and development. Kao, for instance, has about 2,000 of its 7,000 employees dedicated to this effort. GE spent about US$1 million each day for four and a half years to design the GE90 aero-engine. Other companies try to force innovation through target-setting. Gillette, for instance, ensures that over 40% of its annual sales come from products introduced in the last five years. 3M does the same, but aims for 25%.

Value added

Another strategy which hi-tech companies can employ to differentiate themselves from others is adding value to their customer relationships. Some companies unfortunately interpret the term "adding value" to mean making things cheaper for the customer. Price-cutting and rounds of promotions do benefit consumers, but they normally do not benefit a brand's image, and can even bring about perceptions of cheapness. They also lead to price wars in which no company can really win.

In consumer minds, value is not just about price but is all about technology products and services that make for real value, including the brand's value to the user. If companies can establish a perception of value, then they will overcome many of the obstacles associated with price. The value-added positioning strategy is a vital part of the positioning mix if competition on price is to be avoided. IBM, for example, cannot claim to be number one in terms of technology innovations, but what it purports to offer is better service and support compared to many other companies. This strategy adds to the customer's perception of value.

Unlike IBM, Acer Computer shows that it is possible for the value-added positioning strategy to be closely connected to the innovative strategy. Acer Computer has developed the concept of "innovalue"—using innovation to create value in the design and production of cutting-edge products. The positioning of Acer is revealed in its recent corporate mission statement, "Fresh Technology Enjoyed by Everyone, Everywhere." "Fresh" here does not mean new but the best—that is, proven high-value, low-risk technology that is affordable to everyone, and a long life span. "Fresh" also means innovation based on mature technology that is user-friendly, reasonably priced, and enjoyed by everyone, everywhere. Acer Computer also adds value by enhancing consumer perceptions of the benefit or value of its products, based on know-how, packaging, design, accessibility, comfort, user-friendliness, and capability to offer niche solutions.

Yahoo is another example of a great value proposition. It is not just a directory, but adds value to this service by helping consumers with e-mail, yellow pages, stock quotations, and many other valuable sources of information all in one location. And like other great brands, it keeps adding more and more value to the consumer experience.

The overall concept of value is an essential part of the technology brand promise, and has to be part of the positioning mix. The key lies in producing a value proposition that is both distinctive and deliverable.

Combining strategies

Many powerful brands combine positioning strategies for maximum effect. For example, despite the sheer power of these brands in terms of aspirational appeal, Rolex still stresses complete reliability and precision, as does TAG Heuer. There is still a felt need to portray both their rational and technological virility. They take no chances when they ask consumers to pay up to a thousand times more for their timepieces, compared to cheaper brands that keep the time just as accurately.

Commtouch—with its "Does your site have the touch?™" tag line—helps online customers add value to their sites with its Commtouch Custom Mail™. It combines the problem-solution positioning strategy with the value-added one, offering e-mail solutions that give companies the opportunity to turn visits into revenue opportunities by outsourcing their e-mail to Commtouch.

Fujitsu emphasizes its leadership position with its problem–solution capability, saying, "Fujitsu is a global information technology leader offering everything from PCs and servers to software, disk drives, and printers. We're also a telecommunications and microelectronics giant with unmatched expertise in putting together end-to-end networking solutions."

Other companies combine strategies to dispel the fears in the consumer's mind. Take, for example, the airlines. There are only two things that consumers really care about air travel—safety and service quality. The airlines take care of the safety dimension, not by talking about safety, which could create the wrong impression in consumer minds, but by communicating about their modern fleets. So, to say that they have the youngest planes is to point consumers to the relative safety of an airline company and, of course, its financial strength. Service quality, a multi-faceted dimension, is addressed by features and attributes positioning with respect to concerns such as leg room, culinary advantages, comfort, and privacy. The Airbus advertisements are exceptionally good at combining all the appropriate positioning strategies, showing the features and benefits of its new planes being patronized by affluent people, who are shown in a relaxed mood in a modern setting, with a touch of humor thrown in.

Finally, how about the sheer unadulterated use of the emotional and aspirational positioning strategies, as used by Honda? It tells of its re-entry into Formula One racing, with a print ad entitled, "The Power of Dreams." The copy reads, "A prudent person timidly asks, 'Is it feasible?'

A braver one calmly questions, 'Is it possible?' Honda passionately thinks, 'The power of dreams can.' For as long as Honda has existed, we have set our sights on some of the greatest challenges on earth. Higher is not high enough. We scale the peaks. Realizing the technology others think is a fantasy. Entering the unimagined place in the record book. That's what we call a dream. And driven by the power that roars from such a dream, we reach the edge of what's possible."

Clarifying the brand position

We have looked at several strategies for positioning technology companies and products, all of which are useful for looking at how the brand may be communicated to consumers. Let us now consider the discipline of writing down the desired positioning of the brand in a neat statement that will explain why the brand is different and better than the competitive brands on offer. Many companies do not bother to do this, and end up with inconsistent and off-brand marketing communications. Worse, they can end up with an unsatisfactory position. As positioning is concerned with managing perceptions, companies must have a clear view of what they want those perceptions to be. If they position their brands well, competitive brands will lose the opportunity of possessing that particular mental association.

Writing a positioning statement is not an easy task, which is probably why many companies do not bother with it. Yet it is a rewarding discipline. The written expression of a brand's positioning is called, not surprisingly, a positioning statement. Here are a few pointers about how to write them.

Writing positioning statements

Positioning statements contain several things in a maximum of three sentences. These are:
- brand name
- competitive set (main competitors)
- target audience(s)

- strategic competitive advantage (SCA) of the brand
- benefits the consumer derives from the brand, especially the SCA
- brand personality characteristics

There is no one format for putting all these together. Here's one, however, that we have used successfully:

Brand X
is better than
(in this space write the competitor description)
for
(in this space write the target audience description)
because it
(in this space write the SCA)
with the result that
(in this space write the consumer benefits)

It does not matter if you use your own format, or just put everything into two or three sentences. What is important is that you think through the information carefully and express the positioning statement clearly.

When writing a positioning statement, write it as a statement of desired consumer perceptions. It should not be a statement of what you want to be (like a mission statement), but how you want to be seen. It is, in fact, the verbal statement of your desired brand image. As such, a positioning statement should be written in words that consumers themselves use, not some technical jargon known only to experts.

To do this properly, remember to keep the statement benefit-oriented as much as possible. The last part of the statement—the bit concerned with benefits—is probably the most important. Specifying why your brand is different from and better than others is good, but you have to be clear about what this means to the customer. For this reason alone, it is best to do a thorough analysis of customer needs and wants before writing the statement. Isolating the benefits that are more intangible in nature—such as peace of mind—will make for an even stronger position, because intangible benefits are linked to emotions, and emotion is a powerful tool in a brand's armory.

When specifying the SCA, make absolutely sure that this is the single most important reason why customers would buy your brand over others. This part of the discipline is important in its own right. Finally, remember that positioning statements are not written for external publication; they are internal documents meant to guide brand communications. However, they form the essential briefing document for agencies, giving them focus and direction in brand communications and research.

Coming out with a good positioning statement may take some time and needs the involvement of several people so that you can get well-balanced views. It is usually an iterative process, and can take several excruciating sessions before the final product is ready.

Positioning facilitates brand consistency

Another good reason for producing a positioning statement is to achieve long-term consistency in advertising, promotion, and other brand communications. Having such a statement prevents agencies from adopting creative ideas tactically, only to shift to other ideas that may be off-brand. As technology itself is constantly changing, consistency in brand positioning gives consumers the stability they need in relating to the brand. So, while advertising needs to change with new, creative, innovative communications ideas, it should remain true to the brand values and position.

Positioning is a strategic and an extremely important part of brand building. For technology companies and products, establishing a strong position in people's minds takes a brand away from the commodity trap. In cluttered, highly competitive markets, positioning provides the differentiation necessary to answer the two critical questions for any technology brand—why it is different from, and why it is better than, the competition.

Several positioning strategies are particularly appropriate for technology brands, but their combination can secure extremely favorable and lasting perceptions. Positioning needs to be continually reinforced to maintain those perceptions and to keep competitors from gaining the mind share of consumers.

Let us now look at two interesting case studies—one involving Hewlett-Packard and the other Agilent Technologies—which should give us valuable lessons and insights into repositioning an old brand and positioning a new one.

CASE STUDY 1

HEWLETT-PACKARD

Repositioning an old brand

Hewlett-Packard (HP), a well-established technology brand that has been in existence for over 60 years, is currently undergoing brand rejuvenation. In November 1999, the then newly appointed president and chief executive, Carly Fiorina, who has a formidable track record, announced that the company was to spend US$200 million on a global brand campaign designed to reinvent HP and address the issue of brand identity.

Proud of HP's heritage, which lies in creativity and innovation, Fiorina said, "We are a company of inventors." Indeed, the company has demonstrated this brand value since founders Bill Hewlett and David Packard (who developed the first audio oscillator that was used by Walt Disney Co. for its famous film *Fantasia*) started the company in a garage and successfully led it to its creation of the first hand-held calculator in 1972, to the firm's revolutionary work practices. The same attribute has taken HP from its humble beginnings to become the world's biggest printing and imaging company, and the second largest computing company.

A powerful brand never throws away its heritage, but seeks to build upon it. This is the idea behind HP's current brand image campaign that highlights invention as the key brand strength, as the "shining soul of the company." Fiorina said, "We are a company founded by inventors, fuelled by invention, and adept at reinventing ourselves to track new market opportunities. Our new brand will give us a clearer, stronger voice in the marketplace, and the world will get a picture of us that reflects our true inventiveness."

The company wants to reposition itself as a fast-moving technology company that makes the Internet work for people. As the Internet is the epitome of innovation in technology for many people, the connection is there. The opportunity for HP is to make the Internet "warm, friendly, personal, and pervasive," according to Fiorina. She believes that the Internet—still perceived as somewhat cold, impersonal, and elitist, according to her—needs a hi-tech company with new ideas and inventiveness to break the mold. So, the brand identity is not going to change—Hewlett-Packard the inventor—but it will become contemporary through the application of the corporate strength to cyberspace.

As far as brand communications are concerned, a new logo design projects the fast, forward-looking nature of the company, while a complete integrated global communications plan is being rolled out. It is more contemporary, featuring just the company's initials and underneath, the word "invent" brings the key message of invention and reinvention across. The brand message addresses itself to all target audiences. For the employees, it means: "Remember your HP gene—the DNA to invent—that drew you to our company in the first place." For customers, the message is: "Our inventiveness can help you be more inventive in your home and at work." For partners, it is: "We can help you be more inventive in the way you serve your customers." For shareholders, the message is: "We can do better, grow faster and be more profitable, and our goal is to do just that—by reinventing ourselves."

It remains to be seen whether HP can successfully move from having an image of a world-class provider of equipment to being perceived as a catalyst for change in Internet communications. It appears to be doing so already, with many initiatives, including the following:

- The Diversity in Education Initiative—working to strengthen math and science skills for K-16 students, targeted at low-income, minority communities.

- PowerUP™, a cooperative initiative that involves more than a dozen non-profit organizations, major corporations, and federal agencies in bringing computer access to children by creating thousands of technology centers in poor communities.
- The creation of community technology centers where everyone has access to computers and the Internet, particularly those with disabilities.

Hewlett-Packard has never been short on ambition. It firmly believes it can reinvent itself yet again, and the Internet industry as well, creating a bridge across the "digital divide" and bringing the Internet to everyone, thus achieving what Fiorina calls the "total e-inclusion."

The real challenge for the brand is to deliver on its promise.

CASE STUDY 2
AGILENT TECHNOLOGIES
Positioning a new brand

For a company that has a fairly entrenched position, where it is difficult to change perceptions, it might be best to create a new brand instead of extending the current one. This is exactly what happened to Hewlett-Packard's Agilent Technologies brand. The creation of the brand, from its name and visual identity to its market communications, is a good example of how positioning is central to brand success. Using a combination primarily of emotional, aspirational, and benefit-driven strategies, Agilent has taken off with tremendous speed.

Background

In March 1999, Hewlett-Packard announced plans to spin off four of its business units and form a new publicly traded company. The business units included the original heart of Hewlett-Packard—the Test and Measurement business that Hewlett and Packard established as well as the Chemical Analysis, Healthcare, and Semiconductor Components groups.

HP had become known primarily as a computer and printer business. Being one of the most successful companies in business, it was in the top 20 of the Fortune 100 list. But the public was, for the most part, not aware of the critical role these business units played in the dynamic high-growth industries of communications and life sciences. This company, which in essence started Silicon Valley, was not getting full credit for its enabling technologies in high-growth businesses, while highly specialized niche market start-ups were getting both the credit for leading-edge technology and the market capitalization that would enable them to grow.

HP decided to spin off these businesses, confident that operating as an independent company would enable it to increase shareholder value, specifically by:

- providing greater strategic focus on resources and investments
- increasing speed and responsiveness, thus creating a more agile organization
- increasing accountability to shareholders
- providing access to capital markets to fund strategic acquisitions

The businesses in this diversified technology company would have the potential to leverage synergies in measurement science, electronic circuit and system design, application software, and solutions integration.

The branding challenge

As noted above, HP was known mainly as a computer and printer business, but the leading-edge technology expertise of the "HP NewCo" business units, as well as their critical role in the high-growth industries of communications and life sciences, was not widely known. Customers thought highly of HP quality, but did not in general think of the company as being quick-moving. This was one branding challenge HP had to address in developing and communicating the new brand.

Another was the employee perception of the spin-off, which came as a shock. The 40,000-strong workforce in the business groups that were spun off felt like they were being disowned by a company that had always prided itself on a strong corporate culture and the "HP way" of doing business.

Creating the brand

NewCo hired two agencies to develop a brand identity and name for the new company, and a communications strategy for the new brand. The agencies worked in tandem to define the brand. On parallel tracks, because the schedule would not allow for sequential development, Landor created a name, logo, and identity system, while McCann-Erickson created an advertising campaign to launch the brand—without knowing what the name of this new company would be.

HP NewCo was quite a unique company—though a "start-up," it hit the ground running as a US$8-billion company. This unique combination of Fortune 100-scale and stature, strong heritage of innovation, and start-up mentality became the foundation for the new brand. After the announcement of the spin-off, the new entity was deemed to be a smaller, soon-to-be-realigned measurement division of HP. The objective was to position NewCo as the pre-eminent technology company enabling vital progress in high-growth industries such as communications and life sciences.

Agilent brand mission

The mission or purpose of the new company read thus: "Revolutionizing the way people live and work through technology."

Agilent brand values

Several values provided a solid base for the brand:
- *Innovation and contribution*: Inventing and discovering awesome technology, creating new fields of interest, markets and businesses; seeking and rewarding great ideas that are shared, adopted, and applied to solutions everywhere.
- *Trust, respect, and teamwork*: Believing in the power of our diverse, global teams; knowing people want to and will do a good job,

given the proper tools and support; working in a borderless way to fulfill expectations.

- *Uncompromising integrity*: Adhering to the highest standards of business ethics; operating openly and honestly to earn the trust and loyalty of others.
- *Focus*: Prioritizing and simplifying; saying no to what is not important; aligning the organization to anticipate and satisfy customer needs with a passion; concentrating its investments on maximum growth opportunities.
- *Speed and agility*: Capitalizing on discontinuous change with an intense sense of urgency; being agile; acting decisively; stamping out bureaucracy.
- *Accountability*: Doing what the company says; setting ambitious performance objectives; rewarding those who meet them; rewarding those who exceed the goals.

These values appeared on a card given to employees along with a statement that articulated Agilent's role: "We make the tools for the people who make dreams real." This was to become the driving force behind the advertising brief.

The brand name

The new brand name—Agilent Technologies—was created to signal agility. The corporate identity system included a logo, the "spark of insight," and a "heritage line" that referenced the HP roots of the company: "Innovating the HP Way." The name was launched in late July 1999, with a satellite video broadcast to employees around the world. The launch event included a brand video created by McCann-Erickson, which helped communicate the brand vision of revolutionizing the way people live and work through technology, motivate and inspire employees about their new company, and introduce the advertising campaign theme, "Dreams Made Real."

The advertising needed to address several key constituencies:
- business leaders and key decision makers
- investors (after the initial public offering, or IPO)

- current and potential customers and partners
- employees

Agilent Technologies' campaign—"Dreams Made Real"—seeks to capture the spirit of innovation of Agilent and its customers, the visionary engineers, scientists, research technicians, and doctors who use Agilent Technologies tools to create the technological innovations of the future. It also has a very practical component—until these innovations become practical and affordable, they do not represent a viable business or true benefit to consumers. Agilent's role is to enable the dreamers and the technological pioneers to make their dreams—and the dreams we all have for a healthier, more connected world—come true. The intent was to humanize the technological innovation by highlighting the contribution of Agilent to everyday life.

Two levels of advertising were created: one directed to the general business audience, and another to the key trade publications that key customers and prospects read.

The general business audience was not aware of Agilent Technologies, because the businesses that comprise this new company had been overshadowed by the computers and printers that Hewlett-Packard is known for. To reverse this, Agilent Technologies sought to demonstrate to this audience the essential role Agilent plays in the key growth industries of communications and life sciences. Each execution focuses on a story that is relevant to the general public, and articulates Agilent's role in making it real. The intent was to convey the idea that anything is possible for Agilent Technologies—that Agilent is confident of its ability to contribute significantly to the fulfillment of one's dreams using its experience and expertise. "Dream it, and Agilent can make it real" is the message that it seems to convey. What's more, Agilent tools can inspire the dreamers to create even more dramatic innovations.

At the trade level, the intent was to communicate to current and potential customers that everything they value about Hewlett-Packard—integrity, quality, and innovation—will continue, and that the new company will be able to provide greater agility, speed, and customer focus. The trade-level advertising focused on the key issues customers face, and demonstrated how Agilent can help make their dreams real.

The advertising plan

The campaign was launched with the following creative:
- TV and print targeted at the general business audience
  - television
    - "fountain"
    - "genes"
    - "next generation"
    - "heart"
    - "down deep"
    - "go"
    - "raindrops"
  - print
    - "satellite"
    - "ladder"
    - "airplane"
    - "pipeline"
    - "overtime"
    - "road rage"
- Two trade launch ads to communicate the name change and benefits of spinning off into a separate company
  - "marriage"
  - "rollerblades"
- Seven business-specific trade brand ads
  - "On Your Mark"
  - "walk/run"
  - "cell phone"
  - "windsurfer"
  - "levitating"
  - "crowd"

The media strategy

The media strategy was developed as a multi-tiered plan to address different target constituencies. It involved general business and trade publications, and had a 25-country launch to top markets based on revenue.

The U.S. plan overview was as follows:
- event-based with continuity underlay
- timed to peak at launch and post-IPO blackout for maximum impact
- multiple exposures to multiple units net to impression of new brand
  Print
- multiple consecutive spreads
- full-color buyout of *Wall Street Journal*
  Television
- multiple spotting within all launch programming
- heavy presence in high-profile events

The global plan overview included:
- launch in 26 countries within one month of U.S. launch
- global media (e.g., *Financial Times*)
- pan regional media (e.g., *Far Eastern Economic Review, America Economia*)
- local media (primarily general business and trade print publication)

Results of the launch

The initial results of the launch of the new brand were excellent. Some facts worth noting were:
- tenth largest IPO in history
- released only 15% of stock in November 1999
- stock price increased 80% within six weeks
- tracking indicated over 35% customer awareness after two months of advertising, with over 40% in the United States and Europe, and a slower build-up in Asia

- preference for Agilent higher among those who recall seeing the advertising
- well received by employees worldwide

At the time of writing this book, the various campaigns are still underway, and Agilent Technologies is still working hard on its brand.

5

Hi-Tech Hi-Touch Branding Techniques

The customer has always been king, but the wishes of the king have often been ignored. Today, however, a revolution is taking place not just in listening to customers, but in actually giving them what they want. Technology has been the prime mover here, and it has resulted in the proliferation of customer relationship marketing programs that combine hi-tech and hi-touch branding techniques to give customers the experiences they have previously been denied. These programs are becoming prevalent in both online and offline branding practices, and are so powerful that they can transform businesses and build brands within a very short span of time. Technology is the enabler. The end result is one-to-one marketing.

The new world of mass customization

The age of mass marketing is dead. Mass customization has taken over and is here to stay. The advent of new technologies has enabled marketers to do something they have been dreaming of—one-to-one marketing. Every customer is different and should be treated accordingly, but gaining the capability to undertake one-to-one marketing has been noticeably elusive. Many companies claim that they are customer-driven or customer-focused, even customer-centric, but the customers they freely talk about have rarely seen concrete evidence of this claim in terms of unique and differentiated product or service offerings.

115

But this all-too-familiar situation is now changing. In the age of technology, more and more companies are looking closely at their customer relationships. *The Economist*, in a 1998 survey of 200 top business executives, claimed that

- 50% of firms will track customer profitability in 2002 compared to 26% today
- the importance of customer retention will rise by 60%
- 50% of firms will be organized around customer types in 2002, compared to 18% today
- 76% of firms expect high integration of sales and IT in 2002, compared to 27% today

These predictions are coming true, and customer relationship management (sometimes called *customer relationship marketing*, or CRM) has been the catalyst. We all subscribe to the Pareto principle, which states that if 20% of customers are responsible for 80% of revenue, or 10% are responsible for 90% of profits, why then should we treat all customers the same? This is the starting point for CRM—the acknowledgment that each customer is different. It aims to build a long-term relationship with each customer based on that premise. Thus, it is also sometimes referred to as *relationship marketing*, although this term has been misused by some to describe marketing activities that do not entirely reflect the one-to-one premise of CRM, dwelling instead on points schemes like the frequent-flyer programs of airlines. Such schemes do not constitute CRM in its purest form.

While the objective of CRM is to enhance profitability through loyalty and value, it is only recently that technological advancements have enabled marketers to put the concept of one-to-one marketing into practice. The Internet has seen some of the most successful applications of CRM, because loyalty means less on the Net. If customers do not get what they want in terms of convenience, speed, and service, they can simply click their loyalty away. And they do.

From market share to customer share

CRM focuses on the lifetime value of customers, and on selling an increasing number of products and services to each of them. It is concerned with customer share. Clearly, the basis for this kind of marketing, as opposed to the kind that sells one product or service to as many customers as possible, is the development of one-to-one customer relationships. The key driver in the relationship-building dimension is an intimate knowledge of each customer. Technological developments through accessible, interactive, and inexpensive media have enabled this breakthrough to take place, while the marketing communications emphasis has shifted from monologue to dialogue.

Technology makes it possible to adopt a one-to-one relationship with each customer, enabling companies to:

- identify customers individually and address them personally
- differentiate them by their value and needs
- interact with them more cost-efficiently and effectively
- customize many aspects of the company's behavior to satisfy customer needs

For example, in the world of cosmetics, Procter & Gamble (P & G) has gone online with Reflect.com (www.reflect.com), a brand that fits with P & G's usual stand-alone branding model (see color section). While having no clear links to the online brand, P & G has put up US$50 million in funding and made available to the start-up 1,500 scientists around the world. What makes this site different is that it is not just selling already known products—the products do not actually exist until the customer makes them! Reflect.com offers a tailored service that "delights one woman at a time." An example of this is a shampoo which the customer can produce herself, depending on her choice of fragrance and the amount of lather preferred. Even the shape of the container and cap is up to her. The product is even shipped with a label that says "made specially for (name of customer)." Who can resist such individualization?

The site also makes it easy and fun for the consumer. The home page we looked at provided a "Sneak Preview," and promised "Products created by YOU. Delivered to you free of charge in under a week. Unconditionally guaranteed." Logging on requires few details, and easy-to-download pages make the site friendly. Additional touches, such as pictures of Asian models that come up on screen for Asian customers, demonstrate relevance and understanding. The whole look and feel of this site is one of style and simplicity.

Building brand equity quickly

By this process of customization, CRM makes it possible to build a brand more effectively and quickly, because it establishes a personal relationship in just a few encounters instead of years in traditional marketing. CRM also takes brand building one step further by focusing on customers that represent the most value to the company, usually measured by profit, thus ensuring their loyalty and encouraging less-valuable customers to become high-value ones. CRM involves asking the following questions:

- Who are our high-value customers?
- Who are our potential high-value customers?
- Who are our low-value customers?
- How can we get potential high-value customers to move to the most-valuable category?
- How does frequency of purchase relate to profitability?
- What are the opportunities to get customers to buy more of our products and services?
- How can we encourage all of the preferred customers to stay with us and buy more from us?

Importance of CRM to branding

Why is CRM so important to brand building? The answer lies in the customer experience. A brand derives strength from its experience with a customer. A good experience will produce a good relationship and strengthen the brand. Conversely, a poor experience will damage that relationship and weaken the brand. CRM is all about giving customers a great experience, making it an essential part of any worthwhile brand strategy.

The tremendous impetus toward generating a great customer experience, fuelled by technology enablement, has led to a hi-tech, hi-touch battle in the retail marketplace.

Hi-tech and hi-touch—the impact of technology on the retail market

Technology for the sake of technology will not win the war of the brands. HSBC Bank Malaysia deputy chairman and chief executive officer Dyfrig John summed up this idea well: "There is an overwhelming need for more automation in banking, but there is also a need 'to weld these two things—automation and personal touch—together.'" Failure to do this, he added, would result in technology banks without a personal touch for customers. But if we harness technology properly, he said, we can provide a rich experience for the customer, and add strength to the brand. CRM does just this.

CRM is about creating breathtaking experiences for the consumer. Nowhere is this more evident than in the battle for the retail customer. With the advent of e-commerce, an interesting shift is taking place in the retail market environment. E-commerce is attracting consumers by offering them convenience, reasonable cost, and valuable content. These things appeal to people who suffer from time famine, who are looking for bargain prices, and who need information before they buy. But what about the actual buying experience of walking into a shop, looking around, and buying while you are there? Will the traditional retail operation survive?

To be sure there will still be a place for the retail store, with its convenient location and low prices. That is why we are seeing a resurgence of local retail stores, bringing us back to the village or corner stores of yesteryear. But they do not give volume discounts like the big stores. Supermarkets were designed to capture these benefits, but they gave way to hyper-markets that were not so convenient after all. Now market research tells us that overall, shoppers do not enjoy shopping as much as they used to. Traveling takes time, and parking is a problem in most urban environments. This situation forces the large retail brands to concentrate much more on the strengths that they can leverage on in the physical, as opposed to the virtual, shopping environment. They have to make the customer's experience more interesting and exciting.

At the extreme end of this complex retailing continuum, we are seeing the emergence of the "brandlands." Nike Town, in San Francisco, for instance, has 60,000 square feet of space filled with interactive sports facilities. Using signposts as guide, customers can climb walls, jog, and do many other sports-related activities of their choice. Levi's has its own flagship store too, where you can even buy new jeans and then jump into a bathtub to start the shrinking process off. Meanwhile, Harley-Davidson is opening an eight-and-a-half-acre park for people to bike. In Asia, Manchester United is setting up its Theatre of Dreams, which aims to give customers the authentic flavor of the Old Trafford football ground. This type of shopping experience brings the brands to life in a way that the virtual mall cannot.

Coca-Cola is going in this direction too. When asked about the role of traditional advertising in the marketing mix, chief marketing officer Charles Frenette said, "Advertising is just one component of our communication. If we need to reconnect every day, a billion times a day, we have to use all elements of the marketing mix. One could argue that it's probably about 25% of the communications mix for us. Sponsorship, experiential marketing, grassroots activities, what we do inside the store to create theater for the brand—those are the things you will see evolving as we go forward."

The theme of the new Coca-Cola brand communications platform is summed up in this one-sentence brief: "Only the unique sensory experience of a nice, cold Coca-Cola brings a magical delight to the real moments of my life." It is ultimately the experience that makes the brand, and the brand that makes the experience.

In Asia, the hi-tech, hi-touch route is also making waves, as shown by the following examples:

SingTel—the hello! store

SingTel has a sophisticated brand strategy that uses the total spectrum of market communications. Believing the customer experience is critical to building brand equity, the company opened in late 1999 a new flagship store, *hello!*, the aim of which was to:

- maintain SingTel's market leadership
- position SingTel as the preferred service provider
- distinguish SingTel as a total solutions provider

The brand personality characteristics of SingTel are as follows:

- friendly
- trustworthy
- understanding
- innovative
- contemporary

The flagship store's contributions to this personality are:

- the provision of one-stop customer service, with highly professional staff
- a hi-tech, hi-touch store layout, fixtures, and finishes
- a central location with high-visibility store frontage
- the ability to generate retail excitement and traffic through showcasing latest technologies/trends and interesting lifestyle activities.

The actual consumer experience is key to the success of this initiative, so *hello!* provides a one-stop center for all the company's products and services. The store has long operating hours—seven days a week, including public holidays—much longer than those of its competitors, giving customers greater flexibility to decide when to visit the store.

hello! gives priority to customer choice, with products and services available in stock, and all the latest service, product, and promotional offerings. It has planned customer service with meticulous care, utilizing:

- one point of contact for every customer
- short waiting periods
- quick transaction times

- a relaxed and comfortable environment, including a cafeteria
- knowledgeable and friendly staff
- no-fuss browsing and hands-on live displays, e.g., testing mobile phones
- the opportunity to try out the latest technology with no hassle

SingTel did not decide on these details in an arbitrary fashion, but with utmost care, undertaking focus group research to find what customers wanted in an ideal retail store. It also provided tours to other telecommunications outlets overseas to establish state-of-the-art practices. Furthermore, it hired a world-class retail design company to design the premises, in line with its brand personality. It left nothing to chance.

But this trend does not mean that power retail brands no longer need to provide online services. On the contrary, they need an online presence, or they could lose out to lesser-known brands. Most of these brands have managed to do so. For example, Nike is taking orders for customized training shoes online and delivering them directly to customers' homes. Customers can specify the colors and features they want in the models offered. Proof of Nike's earnest pursuit of this scheme was its decision to buy a shareholding in Fogdog, an Internet retailer in California.

Nike, however, was a bit slow off the blocks with its e-commerce initiative, and still does not have its full product range available online. By mid-1999 it found itself lagging behind many other shoe store chains in e-commerce execution, such as Foot Locker, whose Web sales increased sixfold in the first nine months of that year.

ONLINE CRM

The Internet is where the majority of mass customization is taking place. What technology has done for the brand experience is create a learning relationship between the customer and the company. By not just remembering details about customers, but by talking to them and allowing them to interact with you online, you learn the customers' needs and wants, to which you can then tailor your products and services. The wonderful thing about this mechanism is that it engenders customer loyalty. It does so not just by giving customers what they want—which is powerful enough in itself, and necessary—but by making sure that it is more convenient for them to stay with your company than with any of your competitors.

This is nothing new, if we think about it. Small local stores have done this down through time, remembering everything about their customers and their families, learning about what they want to buy and when, altogether giving them a warm, friendly, and extremely personal service. What is new is that big companies, even with huge sales forces, have not been able to do this until the recent developments in computer software took place. This is the reason why more and more consumers are shopping online.

Examples abound of how technology is helping customers to have a better and more one-to-one brand experience. Telus, Canada's second largest telecommunications provider, has a Web-based customer billing and self-service facility. Using personalized billing solutions, the site (www.selfserve.telus.com) has over 25,000 registered online customers, who can enjoy bill viewing, payment, service ordering, and provisioning. Telus also sends powerful personalized messages every month to customers logging on to pay bills, enhancing opportunities to increase revenue by cross-selling and up-selling additional services.

Shop at Home, Inc. sells specialty consumer products, mainly collectibles, through interactive electronic media, including broadcast, cable, satellite television, and the Internet. Its Web site (www.collectibles.com) combines the power of its 24-hour television network and BroadVision technology to harness a fully integrated sales platform that enables customers to interact with the company seamlessly across multiple distribution and communication channels. BroadVision's One-To-One Retail Commerce was successfully linked with LivePerson's customer service technologies, hi-touch customer relationship management software, and their new enterprise systems, Oracle database, Oracle HR, Oracle Purchasing, and Oracle Financials. The site will host a set of features that will differentiate it from other retail sites, namely:

- a virtual shopping cart that stays onscreen while the user navigates and adds products to the cart (so unlike those sites where users have to click out of the Web page to reach their carts)
- a personalized home page as well as targeted offers
- a call center that allows customers faster, more personalized service, the ability to directly track the progress of orders, and the ability to communicate the status of an order through any channel, including integrated voice response and e-mail
- a means for customers to engage in live conversations with customer service representatives
- 3-D technology that allows customers to view some products via 360-degree rotation, and zoom in and out of the image
- dynamic product-driven video presentations highlighting the company's ability to sell in video with Internet commerce

On the business-to-business side, www.e-steel.com provides a personalized negotiation site for buying and selling steel. Users can customize their reach to customers and markets based on existing relationships, pricing structures, and distribution arrangements. Sellers can thus offer the same product to different customers under different conditions—for example, by offering a long-term customer more favorable conditions. Similarly, buyers may send inquiries to one supplier, several preferred suppliers, or many potential suppliers.

The site has the power to mirror existing relationships on the Web. Users will be able to have a password-protected site and a customized home page where they can design profiles, view industry news, weather, stocks, and create a portfolio of the industry. The system will remember their business and track their current negotiations, allowing them to check on the status of an offer and put in counter offers.

In Hong Kong, Tung Fong Hung Holdings recently launched www.altermedic.com and www.fit-express.com. Tung Fong Hung is one of Asia's leading suppliers of traditional Chinese medicines and health foods. *Altermedic* stands for "alternative medicines." The www.altermedic.com site is said to be the first portal in the world to provide comprehensive information on traditional medicines, therapies, and health care practices, with focus on Chinese herbal medicine and health food. Features of the Altermedic site include:

- a one-stop health-oriented portal site with over 10,000 pages of information on herbal medicines from China, Tibet, and Mongolia. Customers can obtain health advice online through regular columns contributed by medical practitioners around the world. They can also locate information about thousands of diseases and other medical problems through an online library.

- an online diagnosis that enables Internet users to key in the symptoms of their illness, and receive an instant preliminary diagnosis with recommendations of therapies, recipes and diets, and an online personal health assessment from a group of professional consultants

- online video chat-room and discussion forum sessions where users can converse with professional medical practitioners on a range of topics such as traditional Chinese medicines, health, skin care, wine, and food

- online games based on knowledge of Chinese medicine with lots of prizes to be won

- personalized versions of the Web site content and background music, designed according to users' browsing habits and preferences

- availability of the full content in Chinese and eventually in Japanese and English.

On the other hand, www.fit-express.com is an e-tailing platform included in www.altermedic.com, mainly for selling the group's products, including Chinese medicines, health food products, and pharmaceutical items. *FIT* stands for facsimile, Internet, and telephone.

The site's features are:

- a provision to place orders by fax, Internet, or phone. Local delivery is made within three days from confirmation of order.

Delivery service to Singapore, Taiwan, and Canada is also possible because of the company's presence in these countries. Customers can also choose to collect their orders at any of the group's retail outlets or sales counters—customers ordering Chinese herbal medicines will enjoy door-to-door delivery of ready-made herbal prescriptions, the first of its kind in Hong Kong.

- a restricted trading section (B2B site), called "Pro-Medic Store" (short for Professional Medicine Store), for pharmaceutical products, which can only be accessed by medical practitioners and pharmacists, registered with the site
- up-to-date market and product information, price discounts, and storing of personal shopping records

The core of the Web site is the result of a strategic alliance between Hewlett-Packard and BroadVision that allows Tong Fong Hung to conveniently manage the content of the Web site and quickly execute changes to support promotions or to respond to market developments.

Companies bringing innovations into their businesses, such as those mentioned above, are asking the right questions before they embark on their online business strategies. The following discussion highlights a few of those questions that need to be asked and answered.

WEB SITE BRAND IMPACT AND DESIGN

The customer experience remains central to the brand proposition, whether the customer is online or not. The principles of branding are much the same. However, there are unique considerations in Internet site branding which this chapter must address.

One of the first questions companies considering a Web site need to answer is, "Do you need one at all?" Some companies think they have to be on the Net simply because it is the thing to do. But once they have developed a Web site, they do not use it to great effect. This failure can be damaging to the brand. Other companies develop a Web site even if they do not need one. The message here is that there must be some real purpose behind your Web site, and it should have a place in your company's goals or objectives.

Questions for Web site branding

There is no point in putting up a Web site just because it is in vogue, or because your competitors have one. Here are some questions you need to ask yourself.

What is your long-term objective?

It is important to get to grips with the real purpose of putting your company, or its products and services, on the Internet. Like everything, a Web site is developed in phases. Your short- and long-term goals will help you determine the Web communications strategies to adopt for your target audiences/visitors. For example, is your objective:

- to build a virtual business or support your existing offline business?
- to provide customers with specific technical information?
- to increase sales, reduce the sales force, or increase its effectiveness?
- to offer customers an alternative channel of purchase/distribution?
- to build a customer relationship management program?
- to attract a different segment of customers?
- to gain global reach?
- to raise brand awareness and recognition?

Any one of these could be a strategic objective that will determine the kind of Web site you should have in terms of audience, style, content, offerings, number of pages, interaction, e-commerce, and advertising. If your audience is not based solely on the Internet, then you will need integrated marketing and promotions.

Aside from having a strategic goal, you also need to gain name recognition on the Net. What is happening today with a lot of Web-based companies is a mad dash to gain brand recognition, because getting established now on the Net is going to facilitate rapid growth as the number of Internet users shoots up over the next few years. So whether your business is new or old, virtual or physical, you really need to get your brand out there in cyberspace, assuming, of course, that doing so fits your company's objectives.

Is your Web site consistent with your objective?

Think carefully about whether the Web site you propose to have, or already have, is really appropriate for your company. For example, if you are selling a basic commodity-type product such as household batteries, will being on the Web increase your sales? It is doubtful. People will continue to buy them at the corner store. In which case, it would be more appropriate to increase your point of sales presence. However, if you are selling industrial batteries in bulk to businesses, then e-commerce could generate bigger profits for you by giving potential customers technical information and allowing them to order online at a lower cost.

Another consideration is that an Internet presence can stimulate consumers to buy from traditional channels through promotional features. Even in this case, an e-commerce capability is not required. But if e-commerce is going to provide customers with massive benefits, you may consider gearing your traditional advertising and promotion toward supporting your Web site. In this light, here are two questions to consider:
   1. Which marketing channel is supporting which?
   2. Is your Web site intended only to extend your brand awareness through brochures, as opposed to giving people other types of information and interactivity to build their brand experience?

Who are you talking to?

You should also give careful thought to your target audience. So ask yourself: Is your objective related to brand awareness or attitude? Can the various motivations be represented on the Web and the message effectively communicated to the visitor online? So much of the brand experience lies within the quality of content and the creative or interactive form it takes.

You cannot be all things to all people on the Internet, just as you cannot in traditional marketing. But you can identify the different groups of audiences who are likely to visit your site, and thus create selective pages and contents to cater to different segments. For example, you may have a more persuasive content in a page targeted at the brand switchers among your visitors. Selectivity and relevance in presentation are key. How do you best present them? If you present them as text, how do you put it succinctly? Can you provide a better brand experience by converting it into a fun and memorable interactive experience?

Many companies just put up a site and hope that millions will look at it and keep coming back. There is a lot of naiveté about that kind of thinking, because getting attention in the first place is not easy, even if people are looking for you. One way to address this concern is to link your site to other sites that will attract your particular target audience. So, think like a customer. What words would they use to search? What sort of brand experiences are they used to? Will visuals or text be more likely to attract them once they get to your site? What are the top three or five things, for instance, that they look for when they click on a site? Once a visitor is in your site, you need to make it clear what he can get from it every time he clicks on it.

People surfing through sites are generally goal-driven and will not want to be delayed by attractive but slow-to-download graphics. Should you keep graphics to a minimum? How much banner advertising will be considered too much of a distraction? Should your banner ads appear on pages after specific tasks have been accomplished? Animation effects such as flashes require plug-ins; unless the message requires them, you should avoid getting the target customers to download the plug-ins. Do you need a myriad of colors on the site, or will fewer colors be more consistent with the brand image? What words will have a better impact on the task? Do they reflect the brand personality?

How can you get customers to stay and return?

Engaging people's attention is one thing; getting them to stay on, or return to, your site is another. This is what is commonly known as the "stickability" or "stickiness" factor. When do people start to click out of a site or decide never to return? Here are some answers:

- *When it takes too long to access the site.* Thus, avoid loading your home page with too much color, too many graphics, or heavy animation. This is the point where visitors find it most tempting to click away. The Ritz-Carlton Hotel is known to have a magnificent site, so we tried to visit it only to find that its access time was prohibitive. This leads us to the next point.

- *When a page takes too long to download.* Practically everyone who has ventured onto the Internet has been frustrated by the length of time it takes to download certain graphics or to shift to the next page. Research shows that the patience level of the goal-driven Internet user is less than 20 seconds. So, even if your branding strategies are right, a slow download will be your site's downfall, because consumers will not wait to get information or complete their online transactions.

- *When the contents are irrelevant.* Relevant content should be easily accessible by your different target visitors. You also have to ensure the accuracy and timeliness of information. The relevance has to be interesting to the target customers.

- *When the buttons mislead and navigation is confusing.* This can sometimes come from complicated site designs where buttons are used in place of words. Plan the architecture of your site from the short- and long-term perspective, and make provisions for additional pages of text and tasks. The most important aspect of navigation and usability on the Internet is intuitiveness. It means you need to understand how your visitors are likely to think and respond. A clear navigation bar with the location of appropriate titles on the right levels is critical.

- *When too many words get in the way of a simple task.* If customers are meant to click on a link that leads to various products being sold online, a simple title such as "Browse and Buy" will be clear and direct.

- *When the search engine in the site is inadequately developed.* This often results in messages like "No search selection found." Even for simple key words such as "returns," this capability should be there.

- *When there is no feedback mechanism.* This is indicative of either a poorly planned site or a brand without a commitment to customer service. Unfortunately, there are many sites without feedback mechanisms. But having one is not enough. Any feedback from customers or visitors should be immediately acknowledged and looked into. And as mentioned earlier, transparency and accountability come with the immediacy of the Internet. If an error is made, speedy recovery is essential. Remember that a Web site is an extension of the brand personality. Tardiness in responding to online feedback reveals a lack of commitment to the Web site and consequently to customers. Another somewhat unpalatable fact of Internet life is that one dissatisfied customer may not just tell ten to 20 people about his unpleasant experience. As research in traditional sales tells us, unhappy Web site visitors may tell thousands about their experience via one simple e-mail.

Design tools to assist your brand experience

Technology tools are becoming available to help companies considerably in bringing their brand to life on the Net and giving the customer a great experience. They fall into the following general categories.

Customization

Some software systems allow customers to create their own very personalized interfaces between themselves and the company. This is still a developing field, but brand leaders like Yahoo are already doing this.

Community facilitation

This is becoming more commonplace, offering consumers the ability to engage in interpersonal communications, and take part in dialogues with others. Discussion boards, rating exercises, and competitions are becoming more widely used. For example, www.brandingasia.com has a "great brands" competition, while its parent site, www.apmforum.com, has discussion boards about Asian business and other issues relevant to the site. Virtual marketing also fits into this category. Virtual marketing encourages one person to tell another person something about your brand, or to interact with others through incentives.

Purchase tools

These are tools that make online purchasing easier, getting the purchase order process down to a minimum of clicks. For example, Amazon.com has a one-click ordering system that does not require the same transaction information to be entered for repeat purchasers.

Self-help

Some companies like FedEx have enhanced the value of their brand by making it possible for customers to perform certain tasks such as monitoring their transactions and accounts. Financial services brands are also using these software tools to allow customers to monitor their accounts and initiate address changes, among others.

Customized design

The facilitation of customized products is also becoming an integral part of the brand-building process, as companies such as Dell have demonstrated.

Encouraging brand loyalty online

There is nothing like putting yourself in the customer's shoes. Here are a few important questions that customers ask when they choose one Web site over another. If you bear these in mind, you will be well on the way to establishing customer loyalty to your brand.
- Can I get what I am looking for quickly?
- If I cannot get what I want, can you help me get it?
- If I tell you what I like, will you remember the next time I see you?

- Can I go in-depth into the content I am interested in?
- Can I meet like-minded people?
- Can I pick up where I left off the last time I was here?
- Can I expect that the information I give you about me will remain confidential?
- If I buy something from you instead of buying from a retail store, how will I benefit?

The future of branding—hi-tech, hi-touch

Mass customization has indeed arrived, and no business can afford to ignore its potential. The future of branding, therefore, lies in the provision of hi-tech, hi-touch experiences for customers. Whether customers buy on the Net or through the retail store, companies can no longer ignore what they want, what they need, and what they say. There is no more excuse not to treat customers as individuals, or for the brand not to have a distinct relationship with each of the customers. This reality has profound implications for how business and branding will be done in the future. Chapter 6 discusses online brand building in more detail.

To end this chapter, we thought you might want to look at the best example we have found of a world-class CRM program that combines great offline and online brand experiences—Tesco.

<u>CASE STUDY 1</u>
TESCO
The brand experience is everything

Tesco, the giant and most successful supermarket chain in the U.K., has a CRM system that is the envy of many. Tesco found, while looking at its customer base for a typical retail outlet, that the top 100 customers were worth the same as the bottom 4,000. It also found that the bottom 25% of customers represented only 2% of sales, and that the top 5% of customers were responsible for 20% of sales. Like many other companies that have embarked on CRM programs, Tesco realized that all customers are not equal! Tesco now measures valuable customers by the frequency of purchase and value of expenditure.

When Tesco says, "Every little helps," it really means it. Its CRM program is certainly one of the best in the world, and customers love it. Tesco has been principally a food retailer in the U.K., in a mature market that has grown little in the last 20 years or so. That Tesco has grown its business at all is a testament to consumer attraction, when the only route to growth is taking market share from competitors. Its CRM program started with the Clubcard in 1995, offering points on purchases and giving a small rebate to loyal shoppers. Dismissing the initiative as nothing new, competitors did not realize that Tesco was capturing valuable information with every swipe of the card and building a powerful database of customers, which it gained through card-membership information.

The card provided Tesco with vital customer information such as what products they were and were not buying, where they were spending their time in the store, and where they were not, as measured by spending. Customers received vouchers for items they liked to buy and offers to explore parts of the store that they had not yet seen. Different lifestyle magazines were created for different customers, and high-value customers got calls from the manager of the store, valet parking when they came to shop, and other special privileges.

In 1996 Tesco created a student card and another card for mothers, with offers suited to their needs. Tesco then added a travel service through a partnership with Lunn Poly, giving discounts off high-street prices. It also combined its card with Visa through the Royal Bank of Scotland, and offered discounts on DIY goods through the well-known home improvement chain B&Q. In 1997 it added a full range of financial services, and the Tesco Direct service. Adding value was mandatory to these functional items so, for example, expectant mothers were given priority parking outside the store, changing facilities, and personal shopping assistants to help them. In 1998, after the U.K.'s deregulation of utilities, Tesco began to offer electricity and telecommunications products and services. Also in that year, clothing was added to the range through Next. By this time, Tesco had identified 108 customer market segments. This year, 2000, a joint undertaking with General Motors allows customers to buy cars from Tesco.

Noting the interest of some customers in the Internet, Tesco also sells online, delivering products to the customer's door, by refrigerated truck, if necessary. Visit the company's website (www.tesco.com) and you get the same friendly look and feel that people get in Tesco's physical stores. Everything is made easy, and you can buy groceries, books, CDs, furniture, videos, and other items, as well as arrange your personal finance. And, of course, every time there is a transaction, the points mount up. And as the points accumulate, more and more relevant special offers and privileges are given. All in all, the company offers great value and a great experience.

The company is now well on its way to becoming a successful international brand, expanding into Asia by taking over the Lotus Supermarket chain in Thailand, where customers can now buy scooters (tescooters) and have them delivered to their homes. But adding value to the customer relationship is still the driving force behind Tesco's success.

As a result of Tesco's efforts to delight the customer, its profits and market share figures rose tremendously over time, making it a prime example of how technology, coupled with a human touch, can provide customers with a great experience.

6

Branding on the Web

It's different!
You hate it because it changes so fast!
You love it because it offers you things you never thought were possible!
You fear it because you do not understand it!
You want it because it represents the future and hope!
You resent it because it is changing your life!
Your kids think it is cool, and you quietly think it is too!
It's a continual medium of communication between your friends!
You have suddenly realized how much you are beginning to rely on it!
It's here to stay and you cannot escape it!
It's hi-tech and it's all-pervasive!
It's the Web and it's going to catch everyone!
It's creating the future before your very eyes!

The need for branding in cyberspace

Branding in cyberspace is important to both traditional companies and those that have started up on the Net for the first time. Many well-established companies have already gained a significant presence on the Internet, using that medium to support their marketing and branding effort, for example, in sustaining dealer networks, and telling more consumers about what they can offer. Traditional companies have to

137

have a presence on the Internet; if not, they will lose sales and customer loyalty to some of the new Net-based companies.

The two main issues for companies today are how to extend their existing brand image through this new medium, the Internet, and how to minimize the loss of business from virtual competitors. If they are not yet online, it may be a matter of recapturing the business they have already lost. Getting online fast is good for traditional companies for these reasons. Besides, their current degree of brand awareness is something they can capitalize on when they go online. Already, powerful brand names can make life very difficult for new businesses trying to break into the market. In fact, the dominance on the Net by the new "Net only" brands is fast reversing, as established brands fight back with new online initiatives.

For the newer Net-based companies, the task is to build their brands as fast as possible to gain a strong position and market share. If they can gain brand recognition before the established players make their moves, well and good. There is only a small window of opportunity for new firms to build their brands, as there are over 10 million Web sites now and differentiation is becoming very difficult. Thus, they have to establish their own unique identity, and gain a favorable image before other Net-based or real-world competitors do so. Developed to their fullest online potential, these businesses can expect a great deal of success, as companies such as Travelocity have experienced.

All Web-related businesses have to understand what customers are looking for, then deliver the value, completely or partially, through the sites. The interactive nature of the Internet allows businesses to retrieve valuable consumer feedback on a global scale; through online surveys they can better distinguish customer categories, which segments are online, what products they prefer, and a lot more. On the other hand, the immediacy of the Web forces businesses to be upfront and transparent about the value of their offerings, and be committed to responding quickly to customer queries and suggestions.

Customers are quick to recognize such Web sites and willingly patronize (positive brand appeal) these sites for the benefits (brand proposition) and convenience they enjoy on and off the site. Thus, today's consumers are progressively choosing the Internet as their preferred channel for communication and convergence. Businesses that fail to understand the significance of offering real-time value on the Internet as part of their branding activities will lose the opportunity to interact and build online brand relationships with all or part of their consumer markets. Branding is therefore critical to the new breed of Internet companies.

The Net generation—a powerful new segment

With the advent of the Internet, new consumer segments have emerged. None has been so marked, and none so potentially important to brand builders, as the segment known as the Net generation, or Generation-N. This generation constitutes today's youth, who have grown up with the computer as a personal aid and with the Internet and interactive media as the preferred means of communication and entertainment.

Generation-N is different from past youth generations. They have a greater disposable income and a greater influence over family purchases because of its superior access to comparative product or service information. In other words, they have the power of influence.

Generation-N is growing up in homes enjoying greater convenience and comfort than ever before. Technology is just a part of life for them, and they are familiar with the electronic world. They are more demanding than past generations because they can have literally everything on demand, whether it is music, movies, information, news, sport, or banking service. They are proactive, not reactive with this power, and search for knowledge as an animal searches for food—on the Net. Working on the computer is not work at all; it is fun, and information is the common currency. Non-Net-related work is boring.

They have an endless fascination with instant, fast services, and have little patience for anything that does not conform to their standards of speed and relevance. Things like bus passes are regarded as passé, while smart cards are cool. They demand choice, and want to pay only for what they use and experience. Generation-N is already buying large quantities of products online, such as CDs, event tickets, books and magazines, clothing, computer supplies, air tickets, hotel reservations, cell phones and pagers, and many other things. They also like to do research and send e-mail, chat and play games, and window-shop online.

Interestingly, researchers are uncovering more information about this new breed of consumers.

The brand expectations of Generation-N

Given the above profile, what are Generation-N's expectations of brands on the Internet? If we consider what they like and want, we will gain an insight into what brand builders are going to have to provide in the online environment. Principally, these are:

- faster, easier, and more convenient access to brand information
- quality services and confidence in products in what is fast becoming a commoditized world
- highly flexible, customized, or personalized services and products, and environments which they can influence
- as many options as possible
- a highly interactive environment
- one-stop services, which they see as a necessity, not an advantage
- aesthetic appeal

All companies have to understand this new generation of people to whom using the Net is second nature. Because they will demand a new type of experience, companies will have to adapt to their needs and wants with lightning speed. Some companies are already attending to their needs, such as Alloy Online, Bolt.com, and Snowball.com, by offering content and shopping for this market, and marketing themselves to companies as gateways to the teen market, signing deals with major companies for online advertising and sponsorships. As Generation-N increases, more and more companies will have to learn the new rules of branding on the Web to attract them.

Online and offline brand strategy—names and trust

For traditional companies, the Internet represents a potentially rich market, but as we now know, Internet customers are different from those of the general population. Generation-N is one major example, but other Net users also seem to be looking for different things in the virtual world, and they tend to be in the more affluent bracket. This has caused some companies to look at different ways of branding to address this issue. Basically, companies have three alternatives in developing an online brand-naming strategy. These are to keep the same brand and merely put it online, create an online brand that is totally different, or create a sub-brand.

If we look at the financial services industry, for instance, we can see how these three options are represented. Prudential, with a somewhat old-fashioned insurance image, decided that to appeal to Internet users in banking, it would need a completely new brand with little link to the parent company. The company thus introduced Egg, an online bank that offered bundles of services including mortgages, a savings account, and personal loans. Egg got 1.75 million hits in the first week following its launch, built an affluent customer base of 550,000 in eight months, and got deposits worth £6.7 billion. However, it did not enter the Internet with its major product area of life insurance, and still faces the problem of consolidating this with its new offerings. The online and offline customer bases are very different, as are the brand images. A new brand is therefore good for establishing brand equity quickly where your existing brand may not be easily accepted, and when entering a new category.

Barclays Bank represents the other extreme, where the company has gone online with its own name, Barclays Online Banking, having confidence in its existing brand equity. The strength of the offline brand was felt to be good, as Barclays was noted to be offering existing customers an alternative distribution channel. The Co-operative Bank created a new brand, Smile, but linked this closely to the parent company, allowing Smile to benefit from the strength and brand equity of the parent brand. Smile is therefore a sub-brand as opposed to a stand-alone brand, gaining significant endorsement from using the Co-operative name.

There are no right answers in the naming game, but it is important to research the acceptability of your brand name to your target audience. Brand heritage is important to some people and not to others, while transparency and friendliness can also prove to be prime drivers. If a company does have online and offline branding under the same name, then consistency is mandatory. Separate brands can develop their own personality and positioning.

Trust is the key

According to research conducted in London for Leo Burnett, and which was reported in the *Asian Wall Street Journal* issue of June 8, 2000, consumers trust traditional company brand names more than new Internet names. It appears that although many dot-com companies spend substantial amounts of money on advertising to gain a high degree of brand awareness, trust often lags behind. The same research attests to this. It showed, for instance, that although the brand Lastminute.com was recognized by 84% of the research population, only 17% of the respondents said they would trust the brand. Brand awareness is important, but this does not mean that people will buy that brand. If this research is correct, then offline, traditional brand names are likely to have an easier time gaining the trust of consumers, and online brands are going to have to work hard, not just to generate awareness but to gain the trust necessary for success. Powerful brands are trusted brands.

The old marketing rules do not apply

The old rules of marketing no longer apply when you are in cyberspace. As the Web is relatively new, there is little market research to tell us what people want. We cannot talk to them as we used to do in traditional survey methodology. The traditional segmentation categories no longer exist—demographic and psychographic classifications do not seem to work in the electronic environment. We cannot see them when they make their choices, and do not know the impact of what we do on brand loyalty.

On the Internet, the term *stickiness*, as pointed out earlier, refers to how effectively a Web site can engage its visitors and induce them to stay or return. It is not an effect of brand loyalty, although stickiness to a Web site may well produce positive perceptions of its overall brand. Studying why some sites are "stickier" than others may help us understand why sticky sites can impact the brand-building effort both online and offline.

Branding on the Web is different

Branding on the Web is very different from the typical consumer branding. With conventional product branding, image tends to be the vital decision-influencing factor. The more you move away from commodities, the more influential image becomes in the consumer's decision to buy. Even with washing powder—to all intents and purposes, a commodity—creating an image requires a lot of marketing effort and investment. When you rise up the scale to prestige items such as fashion watches, then image is everything, and developing brand equity is the name of the game.

When you are branding online, the customer experience becomes more important. This is not to say that it is unimportant in traditional branding. It is very important, but it is not the typical experience associated with traditional branding. In traditional branding, the physical aspects of the product or service form a large part of the experience. While the emotional value is very high, say, of buying a prestige watch, the experience of touching and feeling the watch when you consider buying it is very important.

With online branding the experience is different and highly important. As with traditional branding, consumer interaction with the brand is key, because the very nature of the online process is active involvement. Each online involvement requires the visitor (potential consumer) to actively seek out the brand site. The motivation of the visit reveals the importance of both traditional as well as online media in advertising and promoting the presence of online brand sites. But regardless of the motivation, the quality of the involvement, which is fundamental to the brand-building effort, has to be positive. It is vital to remember the brand's proposition at this point and reflect it on the online experience. For example, if McDonald's promises a "Good Time, Great Taste," its Web site should give its visitors just that—a good time, if not a great taste. Above all, the experience should be relevant to the visitor. Note that while brand benefit messages vary in different media to attract different decision makers, the same messages on the Internet need to be packaged for the right visitors to click.

In many ways, the real-time nature of the Internet encourages transparency and accountability. Organizations that claim to be customer-oriented have to follow up with an online feedback mechanism, and support the service with fast online response. This feature alone will test the efficiency of the largest and sophisticated Web sites. In two separate incidents at the end of 1999, a leading bank group and one of Asia's leading airlines failed to respond immediately to online feedback from an irate customer, taking as long as two weeks to acknowledge a Web-based message. The airline's slow online response was inconsistent with the standard of inflight service, which it claimed "other airlines can only talk about." So, the consumer brand experience did not live up to the brand promise in this dimension.

A framework for branding on the Internet

The same theory that applies to traditional branding—the customer experience makes the brand—applies also to Internet branding. It does not matter whether a brand exists inside or outside of the Internet; all that the visitor is concerned about is getting satisfaction from his visit. Navigation buttons transport visitors across varied information and guide them deeper into detailed pages and flash locations of distributors across the world, and bring consumers to feedback mechanisms, real-time forums, and chatrooms to share their experiences.

The ability to save time on the Internet and the convenience of downloading information is a major concern; the visitor expects it. Hence, the value of any experience over the Internet is relative to the ease and success of the interaction. In the world of the Web, "what you see is what you get." In the words of *the Rolling Stones*, if you "can't get no satisfaction," the Internet is a platform to broadcast your displeasure as a consumer. Needless to say, the better the ability of a Web site to satisfy its visitors, the higher its value, because it draws the line between being an "effective," attractive Web site and being a "useless" one. This is very much a brand experience issue.

However, despite the irrefutable fact about brand success and the customer experience, there are yet no widely recognized rules for branding on the Web. (They are still being written as you read this book.) What is more, it is the consumer that is writing them, not the marketers or ourselves. The instant feedback that comes from Web users is extremely useful in shaping the brand experience they expect to have and which you have to give them.

It is also important to remember that Internet branding is still in its infancy. The Web is not very old, and success stories are not in great abundance. Yet there are already obvious do's and don'ts in relation to ensuring a successful brand experience. Before long, we will see second-generation brands offering new customer experiences. Here are some important elements to consider, with appropriate examples that are generally taken from commercial sites, which point to the relative absence of hi-tech brands on the Internet. These sites illustrate ideas and do not constitute any complete methodology in rating them.

1. *Be consistent with your real-world branding and personality*
In any brand-building activity, offering differentiation is important. Achieving a unique and differentiated site is a function mainly of design, but the content (derived from a set of Web-related objectives) should be based on the personality and positioning of the brand. Avoid indirect messages in general content as well as in advertisements, as they can mislead visitors.

If you are not an entirely virtual company, and already have a brand presence in the traditional media, make sure that you are true to the brand identity that people are familiar with. McDonald's Web site (www.mcdonalds.com) is a good example (see color section). While it cannot feasibly sell French fries online, the fast-food chain of restaurants uses its Web site to reinforce its corporate image, reminding its customers and shareholders of its continued interests and investments in the community and other projects. For more interaction, McDonald's could consider offering games on its site to further develop its brand proposition and improve brand attitudes in an increasingly fragmented industry.

Maintaining brand identity (and, in particular, brand personality) is essential to those brands moving to the Web. The Gap is a good example. With www.gap.com there is real consistency, demonstrating the personality characteristics of being direct, straightforward, very easy, and efficient. It is easy to find and purchase products you want. Similarly, there is visual consistency, with the blue and white color scheme and the rotating 3D Gap bag.

Remember, the Internet is one-to-one, and so there is a great opportunity to express your brand personality and build a friendly relationship. For companies creating a totally new online brand, try profiling your target audience by personality characteristics. Write a couple of paragraphs about that "personality," and then extract five or six key words that are central to its character. This will help you start to develop an attractive set of brand values for your site. Once you have created the brand personality for your site, put each characteristic into action. If your personality is "innovative," then your site should reflect this. If it has the characteristics of being fun-loving or independent, then these also should be expressed via the site so that the visitor experiences the brand values you want them to.

You have the choice of providing an overall look and feel that will demonstrate the personality, or even of building areas of your site that concentrate on one or two personality characteristics. For instance, you could have an area within your site that is full of adventure and fun, using games and contests.

Whether you are a new brand or an established one, make sure the brand personality is totally reflected in your site, whether it be picture quality, tone of voice, sounds, graphics, colors, or content. Brand consistency is paramount.

2. Make things easy

Consumers who click on your site are task-focused; they are searching for model names, dimensions, prices, distributors, range, opening hours—in short, everything that has to do with your company, product, or service. It would make sense to ensure easy navigation to the most sought-after information and transactions, and to avoid placing unrelated information in their paths, though this is easier said than done.

We visited Priceline.com (www.priceline.com), the "name-your-price" task-oriented e-commerce site, to order apple juice. The navigation flow for the selection of our product and quantity proceeded easily until we came to an area saying, "Add the above item to my card and QUICK-SHOP by selecting an item below." A less adventurous shopper would have taken the cue and clicked on one or several of the suggested items, just to add the juice to the virtual cart. We found that we had to skip this intermission and jump further down the page to find and click on the "Add to Cart" button. Suggestive marketing? Yes. Sneaky? Yes. Appreciated? No. To avoid any problems of this sort in the future, Priceline.com would do well to fine-tune its navigation and layout, and present a more attractive personality.

3. Think carefully about your advertising

Advertising has not gone out of fashion with the Internet gathering momentum, as some people predicted. It is still an important means of building brand equity, especially for Internet brands, and can take place on your own site, other Web sites, or in traditional media. Again, we will need to define our communication objectives; advertising may only be one of the many strategies we employ. Is it just brand awareness we are seeking? Or are we hoping to use the Internet to generate a quality database of interested consumers? Similar to traditional communication needs, many of the activities should be integrated and rolled out in progressive phases for a more effective reach and frequency.

As for the Internet, because you do not always know who is reading your banners, advertisement messages should offer clear benefits such as:

- "US$10 off any software title. Over 20,000 to choose from. Software.com. Click here."
- "Free T-Shirt with your first online purchase above US$30. MyPharmacy.com. Click for details."

Assuming the visitor clicks on the banner, always ensure that he is linked to a related landing page. If more information is forthcoming, make it available with the next click. If you are seeking information from the visitor, ensure that a privacy statement accompanies the request. If you need registration, ask the visitor to join your e-mail list as well. As can be seen, the immediacy of the Web shows that every page and level can be leveraged for further audience response.

In addition to understanding demographics and psychographics, you will need to decide on the format (e-mail/directory/banner/exclusive sponsorship), site selection (search engine sites, dedicated communities, specific portals), and features (date-specific, occasion-specific, benefits-specific, action-specific).

The ubiquitous banner may not be the right answer for all businesses. Studies have shown that users quickly learn to ignore most banners, and the click-through incidence is extremely low. However, this is not to say that high click-through rates on banner ads are everything. According to AdKnowledge's "Online Advertising Report: First Quarter 2000" released in June 2000, more visitors go to an advertiser's site and transact (this does not necessarily mean an online purchase) after being exposed to an ad message, even if they did not click on the banner. An implication of this may be that sites that are stickier—due perhaps to rich content—rate higher in perceived value even if they garner less click-through. Alternatively, this may be due to the long-staying impact of excellent creative content within the banner.

Either way, it is critical that one understands the objective of other sites before negotiating to place advertisement banners with them. You can always negotiate for banner advertising space on a reciprocal basis, if necessary. And you can always drive people to your site by offline advertising, as an increasing number of online brands are doing, costly though it may be.

4. Boost the brand experience with interactivity

Internet users, by their very nature, want interactivity. Thus, you can create value by allowing the consumer to interact with the brand in ways that are not available in the physical world. A good example to cite in relation to this advice is PhotoDisc (www.photodisc.com), because it shows thorough understanding of the needs of its different users. The organization, which has cleverly moved online, is in the business of renting out photographic images. Its entire range, which covers topics from traffic to conceptual illustrations, is available online via a power search engine (see color section). To test the site, we entered keywords such as "cellular phone and hand," and were promptly given access to 39 available images, along with their prices. Unregistered visitors are allowed to download chosen images (watermarked) for "internal reviewing purposes."

Instead of merely using the Internet for virtual reach, PhotoDisc has leveraged the media and found partners such as LicenseMusic.com and EyeWire to expand its service offerings. PhotoDisc customers can now find and license music while online, which they can use with the images they plan to choose. They can also purchase thousands of fonts. PhotoDisc will also custom-burn the chosen images onto a convenient CD. The availability of the images with music and font features online gives PhotoDisc customers a sense of independence and control, which is conducive to the online selection process and subsequent order.

5. Use the referral system

The good thing about the Internet is that, unlike traditional retailing, it can offer a massive referral system. People enjoying a good experience on one particular site have the capability to tell thousands, not just a few people, about it. Hence, use the power of the community to help spread the good news about your brand. If users have enjoyed the experience on

your site, chances are they will have no qualms about recommending it
to their friends. You simply need to suggest it to them and provide a spot
for them to enter a friend's e-mail address. The site from Internet.com
(www.internet.com) presents the concept in a clean and simple manner
upfront on their home page:

Headline : Free Newsletters

Version   : [click] HTML [Mon-Fri]
             [click] TEXT [Weekly]

Sign-off : Sign up and Win!!

6. Make sure strategic alliances and networks offer a good brand fit
Link up with Internet businesses that are likely to have access to the
customer base you want to reach. But make sure that their brand does
not devalue or dilute yours. Online activities should mutually reinforce
both brands' positioning, share similar target segments, and have similar
brand values. Take the co-branding efforts between McDonald's and
Disney. The use of Disney premiums and a Disney Cruise Line Vacation
helps to promote the fast-food chain's Happy Meals and its new Big
Wrap! Burger (www.mcdonalds.com). Both organizations picked
partners that enhanced their brand propositions in the eyes of their
consumers—teenagers and young families with children—both online
and offline.

In the case of partners Amazon.com and IBM, we found the former's
marketing messages in the latter's Web site (www.ibm.com), but these
were selectively placed. IBM's home page is strategically focused on
dedicated IBM offerings. We managed to find two different categories of
advertisements for Amazon.com when we clicked on "Owner Privileges"
under IBM's Home/Home Office category. One animated banner, which
appeared with other brand banners, simply said, "Find any book you
want." On the opposite side of the screen, Amazon.com appeared under
a "Partner Products" heading, and offered the viewer the option of
clicking on "books, music or videos." Both are examples of businesses
that not only know their consumer demographics but are able to use
psychographics to serve their customers online.

7. Make your brand easy to find

Getting yourself at the top of the pile when people are searching for certain products and services is part of the awareness solution, because it ensures that customers will easily find your brand when they use the search engines. Though this is usually free, one cannot totally depend on search engines for all traffic. At all costs, avoid services that offer to submit your site to hundreds of search engines at a mere US$19.95. Almost every site with more than 30 pages includes a search engine. And though there are millions of sites, not all will be relevant to your topic and the business of your site. It is risky to subject your brand awareness development to dubious Web sites.

If you are promoting your overall site URL, consider the following:

- *Search engines*: Infoseek, Lycos, Altavista, Webcrawler, Excite, HotBot, Microsoft Search
- *Directories*: Yahoo, Snap, MiningCo, Google
- *Announcement sites*: Netscape's "What's New"
- *Subject-specific submission sites*: Search.com, I-Sleuth, Beaucoup
- *Webzines/Ezines*: The ZineZone, Netsurfer Digest, WWWiz
- *Mailing lists*: Yahoo Newsletter Section

8. Establish trust and deliver on the brand promise

That powerful brands are built on trust has not changed with the advent of the Internet. People will never buy from a company they do not know and trust, and this is one of the major concerns of companies trying to break into e-commerce. Guarantees of privacy and refunds, good-quality products and services, and service recovery are vital to the development of trust and loyalty online.

Though the Web has incredible power and reach, the interface is very often on a one-to-one basis, while the brand experience differs with every visitor. The Web content (conceptual or tangible) must be relevant to engage the visitor in a direct but personal way. An example of two differentiated branding approaches is that of the brokerages Charles Schwab (www.schwab.com) and E*Trade (www.etrade.com).

While Charles Schwab can offer potential customers the professional expertise of a long-established brokerage, E*Trade, which was originally set up to offer online quotes in 1999, cannot. As a U.S. institution, Charles Schwab boasts assets in excess of US$937 billion, while E*Trade's assets amounted to a mere US$26 billion in 1999. We reckon this is pretty good, considering the virtual brokerage is but seven years old. If Schwab promised visitors to its brokerage site "a complete investing experience" that gave their members "access to the same powerful tools as traditional brokers," how could E*Trade differentiate its branding?

We see Charles Schwab, a leading brokerage, branding itself as the definitive full-service brokerage, and E*Trade, with its virtual offerings, as a current-day maverick. The content and tone of Schwab.com is decidedly mature; the home page alone has five references to the word "retire." E*Trade's upfront message clearly offers a US$75 bonus if you subscribe. It also throws in options such as two Tina Turner tickets or 25,000 Delta skymiles. These rewards are telling of E*Trade's consumers and potential customers. The brokerage offers investing platforms that range from stocks and options to banking and retirement financial services. It reinforces its brand value by offering online community discussion groups, chats, and "live" events, as well as underlining its positioning as a value-added brokerage by providing an online bookstore with a constant stream of headline news and market snapshots. E*Trade launched its Knowledge Center in the last quarter of 1999 to help the less sophisticated investors further their understanding of investing strategies and disciplines.

But while Schwab.com has as many as five links to policies on privacy, copyright, account and investor protection, and market volatility, E*Trade has none upfront. The E*Trade site has yet to provide the all-important online bill payment capability. Despite the existence of as many as 100 other online brokerages, which continue to grow in number, E*Trade has already secured its position as the leading online broker in the United States. Judging from its current site, it would seem that E*Trade's ability to deliver on its promises has strengthened perceptions of the virtual brand's expertise and integrity. According to *Jupiter Communications* (September 1998), discount brokerages will control more than 50% of personal finance activity online by 2002, taking significant market share away from banks. It has taken just eight years for E*Trade's virtual broking business to attain global recognition.

9. Develop brand speed, simplicity, style, and substance

The challenge of branding effectively on the Internet is also about seamlessly integrating the elements of speed, simplicity, style, and substance into a Web site for access by visitors 24 hours a day, seven days a week. A well-planned Web site also provides impressive pre-sale and post-sale brand experience. In the case of Amazon.com (www.amazon.com), its visitors are bombarded by book reviews, and constantly encouraged to submit their personal views on specific topics or book titles. Amazon.com also invests millions in advertising, both online and offline, as do an increasing number of established Internet brand names.

Other investments include the addition of a personalized engine in its back-end system to identify return visitors and consequently recommend book titles that reflect their previous book purchases. This tack is not without its disadvantages, as consumers have complained that purchasing one-off book titles for friends has come back to "haunt" them whenever they log on to Amazon.com. Emotional branding is absent, as the site is primarily transactional in nature. However, its being first in the category of online books, and given the millions consistently spent on advertising and promotions—many of which are co-brand or cross-sell strategies with other Web sites—has resulted in successful dispositional "where would you go to get a book online?" branding among its many time-challenged Internet-savvy customers. Established in July 1995, Amazon.com is the Internet's best example of how to manage a successful Internet business without an established brand, and how to build an Internet brand.

10. *Provide accurate and relevant brand information*

Internet users are basically looking for information that is accurate and relevant. In this regard, know whom you are targeting very clearly, and understand what makes them tick and click. UPS (www.ups.com) seems to know this full well. Known for its versatile tracking service through the Internet, the company allows its users to track their UPS bar-coded packages—anytime, anywhere in the world. All the user needs to do is to enter a UPS tracking number on the relevant Web page. The site also offers the user access to a choice of automated self-help activities such as "Quick Cost," "Transit Times," "Pickup," "Drop-Off," and "Supplies."

11. *Look for a unique brand category positioning*

You have to stand out from the virtual crowd before you can gain consumer perception that differentiates your brand from the others. If the brand positioning does not allow for online electronic commerce, there are ways to "push" a lifestyle and achievement message, just as the Jaguar people have done. The message the Jaguar Web site (www.jaguar.com). conveys is consistent despite recent design changes: the car is not about transportation but speed and sculpture. It is to be admired for its sleek body and beautiful curves. The current site offers even more enhancements to a picture-filled screen with barely a hint of the consumer's personal aspirations or family values. Nevertheless, the combination of emotional and aspirational positioning is very clear and well introduced.

There is no rush to sell you its range of Jaguar models. Instead, technology is employed to offer a car-building tool, allowing the visitor to select colors for the vehicle as well as its leather upholstery. This feature is accompanied by a selection of accessory packages together with corresponding prices. An online calculator helps the visitor estimate the loan amount or monthly payment based on a 60-month term. The site uses a minimal number of subdued corporate colors, intimating the quiet elegance of a sophisticated user. The style continues from the home page through to its lower levels, and is appropriate for the ultra-luxury car segment, in keeping with its established brand image. For viewers with a more energetic psychographic profile, the site's pictorial presentation is accompanied by a strong rhythm that strongly hints at the excitement of racing. It is unfortunate, however, that there is neither feedback nor a "Contact Us" mechanism, which eliminates any opportunity it has to create online brand relationships.

Choosing a unique brand category positioning need not be limited. Amazon.com, for example, occupies the category positioning of online bookstore, but this does not mean that there is no other category positioning in online books. Amazon.com is a generalist e-commerce site with a brand image tied to books. This means that one can still develop an online e-commerce site specializing, for instance, in interior design. This could cover design-related products and services such as those on architecture, arts and craft, fengshui, accessories for interiors, furniture pieces, Asian antiques, and mood music.

12. Balance brand sophistication and simplicity

Your brand has to look good and different without getting in the way of the consumer experience. It is possible to be sophisticated yet simple, as the Jaguar site shows. But brand managers need to be aware that not all offline marketing or branding activities can be shifted online without some change or adjustment. A case in point is batteries. If you are looking for these products, you would suppose there is a very little chance that you will be able to procure them through the Internet, as your category need is likely to be urgent. True? Yes. Which is why both the Duracell (www.duracell.com) and Energizer (www.energizer.com) Web sites do not try to sell their batteries online.

Both sites do provide wide and varied contents that cater to the technical individual as well as the home consumer—that is, through product education, brand benefits and features, and games and quizzes for the younger segment. In terms of site differentiation, Duracell has a sleeker look and feel, as it liberally juxtaposes lifestyle-type photos shot in black and white to remind visitors of our dependence on batteries.

Energizer's site is a lot tamer in style, and this is where the brand personality and finesse end. Anyone who has watched television commercials will swear that the pink bunny mascot carried the Duracell name. So, why is Energizer's site peddling a pink bunny? Why is its highly successful "Never Say Die" muscleman of a battery absent from the site? A strategy behind the use of mascots is to stress primary brand benefits, such as the use of Ronald McDonald and Mickey Mouse, but it doesn't seem to be the case here. Despite the glaring anomaly, Energizer appears to have the smarter Web site. Not only did it leverage on the pink bunny icon to reinforce previously developed brand attitudes, it also provided suggestions under the "Products" category, pointing consumers to where they can buy batteries online. Didn't we establish that no one would buy batteries online? Take a look at the recommended sites and you will see innovative co-branding activities at work.

13. *Update your site, refresh your brand*

Immediacy is the value proposition offered by the Web. Therefore, as a rule, weekly information updates are necessary for product sites, and seasonal information updates for retailers, with bi-monthly changes to the upfront look and feel, in keeping with the brand values, of course. Much of the content—delivered in the form of text, graphics, and animation effects such as flash and JavaScript—depends on specific brand values as well as the site's likely segments of potential visitors. The impact of content can be limited by the company's investment in technical hardware and software support. One of Web editor Rod Davies's rules (www.apmforum.com) is "be flexible and go crazy with content but be very disciplined that every image, every piece of copy, and even page layouts reflect your single, clean and simple brand message. Brand messages need to be simple and memorable, but experience tells us that the more examples of your brand identity that are provided, the more the message is reinforced and remembered."

Although effective branding does not depend on a Web site brimming with "bells and whistles," there is nothing worse than visiting a site a year later to find that very little has changed in terms of news and graphics. Such Web sites exist, but these are personal Web sites with no bearing on business brands. You do not have to change every page at the same time, but do make sure that pages are changed regularly.

How does technology impact the Metropolitan Museum of Art (www.metmuseum.org) in New York? When the mere presence of the Internet transforms information into a commodity. Instead of ignoring the Internet and faithfully pushing traditional forms of marketing communications such as printed brochures, museum tours, and pre-recorded guides, the Met has embarked on an ambitious project to develop one of the best Web sites for art lovers around the world.

Launched in January 2000, the Met's first phase of the project saw more than 3,500 pieces of significant artwork placed online. Based on the concept of educating the masses, the Met hopes to share its valuable content by providing detailed access and information for research and learning, as well as stimulating their interest to visit its vast collection. It plans to eventually give visitors around the world complete information and access to its collection of more than two million art pieces. Through its Web site, a visitor can easily create his personal online Met collection, as well as download any famous art piece as "wallpaper" for his computer. It also features an online Met shop, which sells fine art reproductions to casual and registered visitors at exclusively special rates.

14. *Provide brand entertainment*

Entertainment is an integral part of brand building on the Internet, as it enhances a potentially dull experience. Though viewed through a screen, a brand can come to life over the Internet through a myriad of interactive and immersing technologies that include games, animation-cum-sound effects, and other innovative elements.

Ragu (www.ragu.com), the famous brand of pasta sauce, once featured an online game that combined visits to its interactive Web site with visits to the supermarket shelves. The game involved an Italian mama chasing her meatballs. Each time the target audience—young teenagers—reached a crucial round, they had to answer a specific question about the brand or its product. The brand experience was novel to its target audience whose product knowledge and brand attitude developed each time they moved to a higher game level. The brand interacts with mothers by providing free recipes, coupons, lessons on speaking Italian, Italian folktales, and promotions to win new kitchen tools.

15. Be brand-specific—explore Net niches
It does stand to logic that a bookstore can easily translate the same business to the Web. However, one would have to analyze the competition before doing so. While it does not matter that one already exists, you have to be a lot more competitive. In which case, one may consider finding a niche segment to service online, such as focusing on used paperbacks. Which was just what we encountered in Martha Stewart's (www.marthastewart.com) move to the Internet. What does a TV personality like Martha Stewart have in common with the likes of online businesses such as cooking.com and retail giants such as Crate & Barrel? All promote lifestyle aspirations such as elegant accessories for the home, kitchen utensils and cutlery, sophisticated gift hampers, and ethnic-styled home décor items.

In Martha's case, the brand is synonymous with the product (i.e., her styling talent). By integrating a daily program telecast throughout America (where Martha cooks and offers decorating ideas) with a monthly magazine of similar editorial content, Martha Stewart has become the stylist of modern American homes. However, by going online, Martha has become a retailer, initiating an exercise in brand extension. The Web site www.marthastewart.com offers efficient and intelligent electronic commerce and selectively promotes items that closely resemble the natural and down-to-earth tone, quality, and style that Martha fans have come to identify her with. Although Martha is distinctly (strategically, perhaps) absent online, "Marthabymail" displays consistent brand imagery, and skillfully uses tonal quality, which links to the style in *Martha Stewart Living* (the magazine). The site also takes online subscriptions to *Martha Stewart Living* and *Martha Stewart Weddings*. She recently introduced "Marthasflowers" online. Check out 1.800.Flowers.com and all established retailers in homestyle industries.

Nike.com has always focused on lifestyle. Thanks to Nike AIR, everyone knows who Michael Jordan is. (Or should that read the other way around?) Although Nike continues to get the endorsements of big names in sports, the strategy is not as obvious in the main page of nike.com (See color section). The reference to Lance Armstrong is but one of multiple links accessible from the page, which reflects the current lifestyle trends in sports—focused and energetic. A direct click from the home page leads visitors to the online store, the Winter Games, and to pages where they can customize a sports clip as well as order a customized shoe. Access to four sub-sites—NikeBiz.com, NikeTown.com, BrasilFutebol, and women.nikejapan.com—caters to specific consumer segments. That a link titled "Whatever" exists also shows that Nike knows whom it has brand relationships with. The site encourages brand interaction with consumers through two mechanisms for this purpose: "Ask Nike" and "Talk to Us." To reinforce the brand experience and help visitors with their orders and questions, Nike.com has Order Service Reps on hand 24 hours a day.

16. Vary content to suit different users

Technology and the world of skincare, make-up, and fragrance are no strange bedfellows. This probably explains why Lancome (www.lancome.com) has taken its entire product mix to the Internet. The site displays Lancome's entire product range, introduces new products, offers a newsletter, and welcomes feedback through Web-based e-mail. It takes a creative approach to the presentation of product information (enabling the visitor to interact by choosing palates and products, recommending lip colors, and employing qualitative-type questions) to ascertain users' preferences and current consumer trends for continuous product development and refinement.

Several platforms engage the visitor in two-way interaction while enhancing the brand proposition, including a virtual make-up studio, which allows visitors to run through complete palates of its makeup range, a Fragrance Survey, and Personal Consultation that recommends a fragrance and personalized make-up based on visitor input. We were told that these interactive elements will engage various female segments' attention while eliminating the need for make-up consultants at shopping centers. These interactive segments reinforce Lancome's brand value among its users and contribute significantly to sustaining brand relationships with users around the world.

17. Manage brand loyalty

How do you manage customer loyalty in a medium that discourages patience while offering more variety than we have ever known? Regardless of the style of product, loyalty is practised less—at home or in the corporate office—because, for one, we can always find a cheaper alternative. For another, there are the hybrids that promise to make daily life a little better, which we buy and try. Which is not to say that we will not buy the previous brand again; we will, but not before trying a few other alternatives.

How, then, do we sustain customer interest long enough to make them choose us again? Let a commercial icon show us how. Toys, in particular Barbie, have also gone the path of the Internet. Barbie has her own Web site (www.barbie.com), though this also links to the main Mattel site. The concept of Barbie, including her clothes and her glamour, is strategically directed at girls. So, in the Web site, contents are cleverly linked to her long-term appeal to three groups of visitors— the girls, the collectors, and the buyers (probably parents):

- The girls' link navigates to games that are strategically developed around Barbie-extended products, one of which allows girls to create their very own Barbie online. An online poll collects data on trends among the young.
- The online shopping link takes the buyer to mattel.com, which is commerce-enabled for online purchases.
- The collectors' link is where the visitor can retrieve Barbie's entire history as well as view up to 400 different Barbie dolls.

The Web site not only reinforces the brand image but effectively answers the needs of three different consumer segments. It is also used to deliver line extensions such as Barbie software for girls, which offers a makeover for young female consumers and their Barbie dolls, and other Barbie-related toys. Customer loyalty among the collectors may be unwavering, but customer affinity with Barbie's ever-changing persona will belong to the next generation of girls.

On the Net, loyalty has to be rewarded or customers will stage a virtual walkout. As one click is all it takes, many companies are using loyalty or rewards programs to keep customers coming back, and thus create long-term relationships with them. The key to this area of activity is to reward people with things that make a difference, not just one-off promotions that cheapen your brand and send consumers looking for a better deal. Remember that the Internet makes it so easy for people to compare competitive offerings, and that universal incentives such as cash and points schemes are not effective as loyalty builders.

Private branded loyalty schemes built around product lines such as the Hallmark Gold Crown Club concentrate on rewarding the high-value customers.

18. Use the Net for brand extension

Some traditional manufacturing companies are embracing the Internet as a marketing tool, while others are still reluctant to do so. Kraft Foods, which has over US$17 billion in sales, has taken the plunge with www.kraftfoods.com. It also spends a lot of dollars to promote, via this medium, the role Kraft plays in helping families bond by means of food. Kraft has been promoting this positioning for some time, but the interesting thing is its use of the site (see color section). Instead of using the site as a place for consumers merely to gain information about its products, kraftfoods.com functions as a brand itself, with the aim of giving its target audience—mainly mothers—"Real help in real time," which is the tag line of its recent campaign.

In addition to online advertisements and partnerships with other marketers, Kraft Foods uses traditional TV and radio advertising to entice visitors to the site. Here they can find personalized solutions to meal dilemmas, e-mail recipes, online chats with celebrity mothers, and recipes using ingredients that are available in their own kitchens. The site then becomes a meal planning product/service, while the company positions itself as one that understands the needs of today's consumers.

ADVERTISING AND PROMOTION

As with traditional branding, advertising and promotion are key to the building of a brand and to driving sales. On the Internet, this is left to your creativity. Some general modes of advertisement include:

- *Banner advertising*

  Banner advertising was one of the first ways by which companies gained access to different Web site audiences. It has since become a spectacular failure with response rates down to single-digit figures, much like traditional direct marketing. Few consumers are actually clicking on them. If you are going to use banner advertising, make sure that you give more than a snapshot of your brand or your promotion. As mentioned before, keep your message clear and your offer direct. Banner sizes and costs vary from site to site. Generally, you will be required to conform to a specific gif size to prevent slow downloads on the site. Like any other form of advertising, people only pay attention to products and promises that are relevant to their needs.

- *URL circulation*

  One simple method of advertising and promoting your brand is to make sure your domain URL is seen on as many relevant sites as possible—provided it is relevant to the audience you are after. The only rule here, apart from relevance, is to obtain as many locations as possible for your brand URL. Yahoo and Hotmail, for example, make sure that every e-mail from every customer contains their respective URLs.

- *Site links*

  One extremely effective way of getting your site known to the right audience is to build alliances with other sites that reach your type of customers, and establish links that allow a person to click through straight to your site. This is more effective than banner advertising, which essentially only allows a "commercial," as opposed to a "comprehensive" look at what you can offer.

- *E-zines*

  Electronic newsletters, or e-zines, are successful one-to-one interactive marketing tools, made possible by the Internet. More than 100,000 of them are published regularly. The soft-sell approach of e-zines undoubtedly moves products, as many companies have found out.

- *Offline advertising*

  We are now experiencing a flood of dot-com advertisements, and it appears that offline advertising is the key to the generation of online traffic. Many cyberbrands are now trying to secure their desired positions, and attract new customers with TV, radio, print, and outdoor advertising campaigns. Many of the enlightened market-driven companies are getting traffic to their Web sites by using traditional integrated advertising, sales promotion, public relations, and packaging. The main thing that separates the good from the bad in offline advertising, though, is that the effective ones do not just append the URL to a normal advertisement; they make advertisements focused on the Web site itself. The idea behind this communications strategy is that by the time people go online they already have brand awareness. If they go to your site, then they are really interested, and you can capitalize on that more easily than if they stumble across your site. In 1999 it was estimated that Web brands were spending between US$6 and US$10 million on this kind of traditional advertising, double what they spent in 1997. Research by Forrester indicates that by 2004, online advertising spend will grow to US$33 billion.

- *Radio and billboards*

  Internet businesses are now using radio and billboards more to achieve the brand awareness levels necessary to drive people to their sites, as opposed to other advertising media. But this, too, can be expensive, particularly for start-ups with modest budgets.

- *Sponsorship*
  Sponsorship has gained ground in brand building on the Net where banner advertising has lost it. Forrester Research says that 28% of U.S. media advertisements in the first quarter of 1999 was based on sponsorships. When correctly targeted, they can be great brand builders. An example is Gatorade's sponsorship of nfl.com and nba.com.

- *Microsites*
  Paying for and managing part of another company's Web site can also help build up your brand with a specific target audience.

There are many more examples of how one can effectively advertise or propagate a Web site successfully, and a lot more issues that can affect the quality of each brand experience. Further research can be made into what kind of advertisement works best for your industry. From the above observations, it would seem that there is room for improvement even for established global brands. This is especially so for branding on the Internet, which involves the interaction of consumers with online content that best personifies a brand's image, personality, and propositions. Whether your business is online or offline, you will need to consider integrated forms of communication to reach the different audiences.

All in all, it appears that building an Internet brand is an expensive business. Robinson Humphrey (a subsidiary of Salamon Smith Barney) has estimated that AOL spent US$2 billion to build its brand, while Yahoo spent US$300 million. This begs the question of whether it is all worth it. As of now, the results are not very impressive. For many investors, the jury remains out.

The brand success factor is still the experience

All innovations in online brand building are aimed at giving customers an experience that will be good enough to keep them coming back for more. What is not unique about Internet branding, as you no doubt will have realized by now, is that whether the brand succeeds or fails depends on the experience enjoyed by the consumer. Providing a great online experience is therefore crucial. When compared to traditional brand building, online brand building perhaps shows even more clearly that the experience *is* the brand. In some ways, it is easier for companies to control and develop the customer experience because they can control all the customer/brand interactions, whereas in the offline environment this is difficult, if not impossible, to do. The development of new and improved software applications will continue to revolutionize twenty-first century brand building, especially on the Internet.

Let us now look at some examples of well-branded Web sites, and learn valuable lessons from each.

CASE STUDY 1
AMAZON.COM
Extending the brand through strategic alliances

Amazon.com is possibly the most famous and talked-about brand on the Internet. It is typical of the companies that confound all normal business valuation principles by achieving a higher and higher market capitalization at the same time as remaining in the red. The company has a remarkably positive brand image, being the first in its category to venture into the e-commerce market, and successfully at that. Its incredible early success became possible through its "Eyes" program, a customer relationship marketing program that notifies buyers via e-mail of books they can buy; and through its referral marketing program that allows anyone with a Web site to earn commissions from book sales and reviews.

In a short span of time, Amazon.com has extended its brand to cover many other product categories. From books it moved on to toys, and later on to diamonds and other luxury goods. In December 1999, Amazon.com bought around 16.6% of Ashford.com Inc., valued at about

US$133 million. This deal allows Amazon.com's 13 million-strong customer base to buy luxury branded goods such as diamonds, watches, designer jewelry, leather accessories, and pens. Top brands such as TAG Heuer and Montblanc are also available for purchase from the site.

While Amazon.com gets the opportunity to take more money off each customer, it also enjoys access to the richer segments. It is moving very much in the upmarket direction with this investment, and has the chance to capture more of the "mass affluent" segment—that is, people with more than US$1 million in assets. This market segment is growing fast, with an estimated average order of as much as US$500, according to Ashford. Analysts said that about 48% of affluent households (with over US$750,000 in assets) use the Internet. They are among Amazon.com's targets. For Ashford, it is Amazon.com's e-commerce brand image that attracts buyers. "We're very excited about working with the leader in e-commerce," said Ashford spokesperson Kenny Kurtzman.

Amazon.com's vision, according to its spokesperson Paul Capelli, is no longer to be just the "World's Largest Bookstore" but "the place where people can find and discover anything they want." This is a somewhat broad business positioning—one which may never be achievable—but one which they are pursuing just the same with alacrity. In this new digital world, who knows what can happen? Already, the company has a customer base of over 13 million people, which is larger than the population of areas like Greece and Hong Kong.

In a recent development, cars have been added to the Amazon.com product list, by an arrangement to host Greenlight.com—a site that offers car-buying services, from shopping to financing and trade-in options. Other recent alliances include online pharmacy Drugstore.com, pet supply store Pets.com, and digital audio seller Audible Inc.

CASE STUDY 2
JAGUAR
Great corporate branding on the Web

The Jaguar site is a great example of branding. It demonstrates that great branding on the Net need not be too fussy. You do not have to fill the pages with graphics and content. Jaguar has kept its site clean and simple, while exhibiting a subtle sophistication. It oozes class.

The marque is always to the fore—the leaping Jaguar or the Jaguar face. This is most important for automobile branding, especially luxury cars. The marque has astonishing value. In some markets, buyers are charged a few hundred dollars more if they want the leaping Jaguar on the bonnet of their vehicle. There is no need for Jaguar to place pictures of cars on the home page, which is so cleverly constructed the viewer can visualize the models in his mind. The absence of models adds mystery and romance to the consumer experience.

The droplets of water lend sensual presence and a sense of powerful, safe, outdoor performance. The Jaguar style—exhibiting understated power, elegance, and prestige—and the sense of affluence are manifest throughout the site. The page is organized to make it easy for visitors to find what they want, be it related to the company, specific models, accessories, or merchandise. The rational and emotional elements combine so successfully to make the visitor want to take the next click to see more. When you visit other pages, you can learn about the Jaguar heritage and racing, and see virtual reality cars. A classic piece of branding from a famous brand name.

[Site brand strengths: Brand personality and positioning clearly portrayed, clarity, rational-emotional brand experience, ease of use, and sophistication.]

CASE STUDY 3
VIRGIN
Excellent brand proposition

Virgin is a catchy name. Unlike the thoughts its name tends to evoke, its brand personality conveys such attributes as fun, hip, confident, winner, adventure, creative, and intelligent. These are about the same terms we would use to describe its Internet site as well. Which is why we say Virgin has got a firm grip on its brand image and proposition. There is nothing complicated about the site design, which is appropriate in view of the wide range of Virgin businesses being represented. The use of colors, which are fairly upbeat, is discretionary. The sub-level topics are presented upfront on the home page, so you know what is available on the subsequent levels. Yes, it could look sleeker, but is this necessary? The pictures are acceptably hip and the text clear enough for us to venture into level 2.

Who could resist not clicking on the Virgin Atlantic site after we heard about the airline and its merger with Singapore Airlines? We clicked on the site to find out what New Upper Class meant, and this was where the "bells and whistles" appeared. The look and feel is definitive JavaScript, which is pretty cool (brand personality) in some quarters. We felt, however, that there was a tad too many heavy graphics which caused the site to drag. We went far enough to view Virgin's higher standards of service and comfort, such as eating whatever we fancied. An element of fun (brand personality) is their reference to the "Cyber Espionage Centre," which invites visitors to "report back" on their findings. The design made the JavaScript presentation worth the wait, but we believe this can be downplayed.

We checked out Virgin Wines and discovered that it would be up and running soon. There was nothing else to access on the site, except for a treat in the form of a £10 voucher for our next case of Virgin wine, for which an e-mail registration was sought, and which we happily provided. We thought this a subtle yet classy little gesture, and it made us remember Virgin Wines. This was not exactly a sticky situation, but we will return.

We got a peek at Virgin Mobile and found that the folks here knew exactly how to treat online buyers—with a lot of respect for their intelligence. No blinky banners, no floaty interstitial. Just simply written features alongside a picture of the cellular phone. It helped that the text was straightforward in tone, albeit a little cheeky, but we already expect that of Virgin—thanks to all that publicity by Richard Branson.

[Site brand strengths: Single-minded proposition, content reinforces personality, hip, and relaxed.]

CASE STUDY 4
HARLEY-DAVIDSON
Effective dispositional branding

Was there a period in your past when you associated a particular brand with macho war veterans in dark glasses, leather jackets, and boots? Thanks to television, we did. Whatever it was that sent men the way of the Harley, we reckon the same is happening today. Something has to be said of a brand name that has so much impact on its consumers they tattoo it on their body parts. The Web site design and layout is very much influenced by the logo that nests atop the screen. We know for a fact that the home page has not changed in a year but note that the pictures have, together with a new line that says the roadstore is open for browsing. Upfront, we can read monthly Harley.com updates and know that we can buy Harley items online.

We read that Harley-Davidson has been named official provider of motorcycles for the 2000 Olympic Games in Sydney, Australia. This piece of news instantly roots its brand image and association, as well as our brand attitude toward it. The brand proposition seems simple. Here is a product that is almost an institution, and riding it will be *the* experience of a lifetime. Clicking and entering "Product" almost reminds us of our Jaguar visit—all models are available for viewing even in 3D— except that in Harley.com, we sense that the Harley experience is about

long journeys, physically and metaphorically, where man meets nature
and himself.

Although there is the Harley family and special rallies for Harley
owners, the brand attitude is emotional and absolute. From a branding
perspective, www.harleydavidson.com should continue to update its site
as a means of communication. Which is why, although the site
emphasizes that Harley owners prefer "face-to-face" chats, their "How to
Reach Us" (which comprises mere telephone contact numbers) should
be taken online as well. (See color section.)

[Site brand strengths: Community-focused, dispositional branding
experience based on emotion.]

CASE STUDY 5

MICHELIN
Comprehensive branding

Did you know that the Michelin man is called Bibendum, and that he
is a hundred years old? Remember, you read it here. Believe it or not, the
tire technology Michelin site feels family-oriented. Its contents are
extensive, and tire information relates to uses from aerospace to bicycles.
The comprehensive site tracks visitors' countries of origin, and offers
them their local time. There are games for children, with the entire
product range available online. As is its archive of innovations, for
which works are in progress.

The site provides access to information on its tires in the Tire Guide,
updates in the world of racing, its travel publications, and its boutique.
Besides its tires, Michelin is famed for the Michelin Restaurant Awards
in Europe, which it created to promote driving in the region (see color
section). An interactive system helps recommend routes between any
two given cities in Europe, after which the selected Michelin route maps

are sold online. There are online demos on computing distances, preparing routes, and choosing accommodation. This is doubtless an established authority on travel in Europe whose value-added services are extremely useful for motorists who love traveling on an open road.

Planning a trip? You may check out the interactive tire selector that recommends particular tire models based on visitor input, and a dealer locator with mapping capabilities to better guide visitors to the location. The site carefully segments its content according to user requirements to help visitors focus on an area of information.

The site is extremely well planned. However, although the home page states that it is the U.S. site, much of the traveling-related information is focused on Europe. There are also several links that do not work, which is a pity. The site has managed to offer several brand associations in its pages, but much of the truly valuable information is Europe-related.

[Site brand strengths: Comprehensive, task-focused, ease of use, and sophistication.]

CASE STUDY 6
DELL
Functional branding

Much has been said and analyzed about www.dell.com, mainly due to its unique value proposition for its customers back in the 1990s—that is, to configure and assemble their very own computer at a low cost. We decided to visit Dell to analyze its site from a branding perspective.

The home page is, by default, related to the United States. The "Choose a Country" request bar is a little overshadowed by the Welcome message, and could do with an improvement of its size or a change of color for more differentiation. We clicked on "Singapore" and were immediately linked to a similar-type interface that was identified as Singapore. On clicking "Home/Home Office", our eyes were caught by four very special headlines: "Why Buy from Dell," "Dell Affiliates

Program," "Great Software Pack Offer," and "Dell-Visa Online Promotion." This was good from the promotional perspective. However, the "Ready to Buy" graphic should have been placed in the central frame of the screen, possibly below the picture of Dellware. We scanned the top frame and the lower frame before we moved our attention to the left frame (see color section).

We like the site for its functional interface, because the navigational buttons are repeated all over the screen, and we know that users have very specific tendencies toward button searches. As far as branding goes, the Dell name is repeated often enough. In terms of the functional experience, navigation is efficient. However, the content could become a lot more interesting with references to users' testimonials on specific products, for instance. Aesthetically speaking, the site architecture is neat, creating a sense of site efficiency.

[Site brand strengths: Strong brand proposition, rational experience, ease of use, and functional site.]

Reflect.com from Procter & Gamble offers a tailor-made service that "delights one woman at a time".
www.reflect.com (refer to p. 117)

Source: Courtesy of Reflect.com. Used with permission.

McDonald's presents an online image consistent with its corporate and brand identity.
www.mcdonalds.com (refer to p. 145)

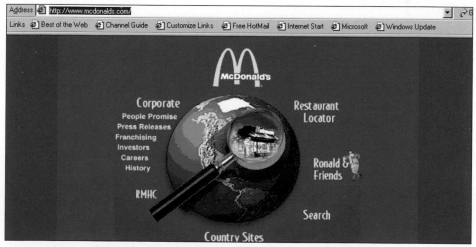

Source: Courtesy of McDonald's Corporation. Used with permission.

Enhancing brand experience with interactivity – PhotoDisc understands the needs of its various users.

www.photodisc.com (refer to p. 149)

Source: Courtesy of Getty Images. Used with permission.

Lifestyles and trends form an important part of the Nike Web site.

www.nike.com (refer to p. 159)

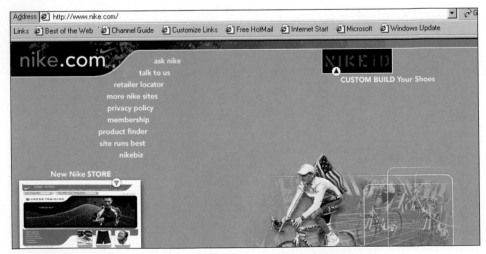

Source: Courtesy of Nike, Inc. Used with permission.

Using the Net for brand extension – Kraft Foods have moved on from traditional marketing tools.
www.kraftfoods.com (refer to p. 161)

Source: Courtesy of Kraft Foods, Inc. Used with permission.

Effective dispositioning brand – Harley-Davidson.
www.harley-davidson.com (refer to p. 169)

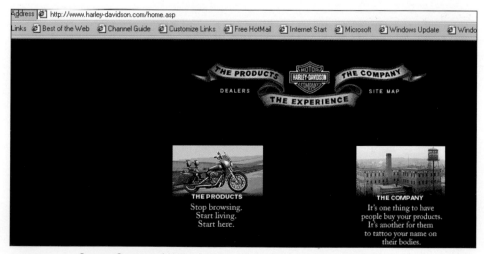

Source: Courtesy of Harley-Davidson Motor Company. Used with permission.

Comprehensive and easily-assessed branding – Michelin.
www.michelin.com (refer to p. 170)

Source: Courtesy of Michelin Group. Used with permission.

Strong brand proposition – Dell Computer Corporation.
www.dell.com (refer to p. 171)

Source: Courtesy of Dell Computer Corporation. Used with permission.

7

The Importance of Branding to Hi-Tech Service Companies

Having already seen how important branding is to technology companies, we now turn to its relevance to companies in the technology services field. As the range of technology products grows ever faster, so does the range of services. Many new hi-tech businesses have sound concepts as a base, but they need the service professionals to help them achieve their goals. The market for technology services is also very cluttered now, and achieving recognition is becoming more difficult. In this light, branding is even more important to these players, not just to be able to stand out from the crowd, but to instill an element of trust and confidence into the consumers, considering that what they are selling are intangibles

This chapter draws heavily on the experience of the National Computer Systems (NCS) of Singapore, which offers hi-tech services. It is admirable for its attainments of success amid privatization, its vigorous efforts to change entrenched perceptions about its past, and state-of-the art services and a friendly but hi-tech brand culture. The brand-building efforts of NCS are recorded as a case study in the book *Branding in Asia*, but the rules and guidelines suggested here were derived from its recent experiences.

Services in hi-tech business

Broadly speaking, the services in hi-tech business can be grouped by service value contribution as follows:

- *Consulting services.* These include redesigning client companies' business processes, charting the direction of their IT and telecommunications systems, and implementing effective methodologies to ensure the highest quality of standards. Specifically included in this category are services such as strategic information communications planning, business and strategy consulting, quality management consulting for hi-tech solutions, and technology security consulting.

- *Integration and development.* Companies in this category design, develop, and integrate computer and communications systems, and provide industry-specific and process-centric IT services. Examples of such services are the development of computer programs for CRM, operation of supply value chain and enterprise resource planning, financial and human resource management, GroupWare and messaging, managed network, smart card/access management services, geographical information system, and e-commerce solutions.

- *IT management outsourcing services.* This category covers a full range of IT management outsourcing services, including the maintenance of the day-to-day technology applications for enterprise, data center and processing services, business recovery services, and call center services.

- *Business process management services.* Companies in this category help clients manage their human resources and supply value chain, and design loyalty programs for them.

- *Education and training services.* This classification involves technology knowledge management and training services in the use of technology.

Notwithstanding their varying services, most hi-tech service firms have the same corporate mission: to create business value for their customers. As the marketplace for hi-tech services is getting as cluttered as that for technology products, branding is becoming more critical to achieving differentiation.

Brand the company, not the service

A growing number of companies in the traditional consumer markets are moving away from product branding toward corporate and house branding for reasons that were discussed in Chapter 2. Similarly, in the hi-tech service industries, there seems to be a trend toward the use of house names with generic services and away from the sub-branding of individual offerings. Trendy naming conventions that treat each new service packaging scheme or offer as a whole new campaign theme appear to be waning in popularity as well. It is easy enough to understand why all this is happening: the cost of creating a brand identity for each new rollout is prohibitive, while the brand equity built through the repetition of one icon, one promise, and one message is either never achieved or lost.

The corporate and house levels of branding are certainly more important than product branding for technology services companies, because reliability, trust, and reputation are key customer decision factors. Also, specific offerings are generally configured for specific clients so that identifying a sub-brand may not be feasible. Hewlett-Packard, for example, does not have sub-brands for its various e-services offerings; it uses e-services as its overall Internet services brand, since its solutions are unique to each of its software, hardware, services, and support systems provided by business partners.

It is interesting to note that for HP, its e-services business started off as a concept which continuously evolves to meet the changing needs of the marketplace. This is in contrast to Lotus, which shares brand equity with its sub-brand Domino. The product Domino is very closely linked to Lotus—a conscious decision to promote both brands together. Both Lotus and Domino are well-defined products with services provided on top of them. HP's e-services, on the other hand, have less well-defined or ever-changing offerings, and where this evolving business model is favored, it is better for service organizations to brand at the corporate rather than the sub-brand level.

Service brand positioning

The IT services industry has already seen segmented players positioned as outsourcers, integrators, consultants, enterprise partners, and solution providers. The basic foundation for service marketing activities may well be the fulfillment of a promise of value to customers. In the services business, the promise of value often has as much to do with the brand itself as the services offered. Nevertheless, delivery on that promise is critical if a company is to differentiate itself from its competitors and stake a solid claim in its target market.

Making promises to customers is what strategic positioning is all about, and various positioning strategies are available to hi-tech service brands, as discussed in Chapter 4. Various positioning strategies are needed to stand out from the competition. For technology service companies, the promise of a one-stop/non-stop service used to be the positioning strategy of companies wishing to give their customers "peace of mind." Customer expectations have made this an industry norm of behavior. Now the most popular positioning theme appears to be "providing solutions," posing difficulty yet again to those interested in differentiation.

Also, at the risk of being repetitive, it is important to remember that a company cannot gain customer acceptance simply by making a promise. It must first determine what promise to make, to whom, when, and how to fulfill it. No business can promise everything to everyone. Making a realistic promise to customers requires the ability of the service provider to assess the potential of relevant technologies and services and to anticipate its customers' current and future needs, even before they can articulate them. This means that marketing, delivery, and research teams must work in synergy.

Power through brand service extensions and associations

As with the traditional branding models, it is more difficult and costly to build and maintain several brands in the hi-tech world, and easier to extend one brand, or stretch it, to cover more than one product or service. It also makes sense to take advantage of the strength of an already successful brand to gain consumer acceptance of a new one fast. The same arguments apply to the service dimension.

Brand extension opportunities

Brand extensions, or stretching the brand name to cover different types of products and services, usually focus on related services within a family of offers. They can span narrow fields of product support services and computing environments such as desktop services, or include entire company portfolios from traditional to professional services. Brand stretch may be limited to product ranges, yet it can apply to a strong service brand that can utilize many different product families through bundling. With technology services, the solution it affords the user tends to matter most, and the ability to extend the brand is greater. A trusted service brand name can even eclipse the individual product brands used in creating the solution. This is the aim behind the IBM e-business service branding—to provide such a strong parent brand name that consumers will have peace of mind regardless of which brands of technology products they use in generating the business solution. The service name thus becomes the decision-making factor, and it is at this level that the branding game is won where other service brands can also use similar products in their solutions.

IBM promotes e-business heavily (it started with a US$200-million marketing and advertising campaign) without promoting the individual products or components that go to create the solutions. Instead, it focuses on positioning IBM as the company best able to take businesses into the new economy, regardless of application.

Adding the service dimension to technology brands

Strong associations between the brand and the consumer define the greatness of a brand. At the heart of strong brand associations is the personality. Since around two-thirds of the IT service providers offer technology products as well as services, service brands need to be relevant to the whole company value proposition. What many product-oriented companies appear to know is that the secret to a lasting company image lies in the personality and promise associated with that company.

Products do not have much personality and are difficult to differentiate in the hi-tech industries of today. In contrast, services, which are delivered by people, are the basis for developing meaningful relationships with customers. So, adding a service dimension to the product value proposition broadens its emotional appeal, helps to differentiate the offer by creating a more attractive solution, and provides the basis for establishing a brand personality association unique to each company. So, as companies such as IBM and HP have demonstrated, adding services lends considerable power to the brand.

Challenges in service branding

Creating and managing a powerful services brand is not easy, given the many challenges to overcome.

The branding of services is often regarded as more difficult than the branding of products, because of the intangible nature of the service business, and the little tolerance for error in hi-tech services marketing. In fact, because of the relatively complex and expensive nature of hi-tech services, and some customers' fear of technology, creating a successful brand for hi-tech service companies is even more problematic. There are many challenges that service companies have to deal with in building a strong brand. These are mainly the following:

- branding intangibles
- managing comparisons
- managing client expectations
- managing multiple partnerships and co-branding
- managing customer relationships
- managing service quality
- building the brand culture
- branding and change management
- managing brand communication

Branding intangibles

The most obvious advantage products have over services is they can be photographed, demonstrated, touched, and easily compared with competing products based on physical attributes. In short, they have tangible benefits. Services are different, as promises involving their potential benefits are often difficult, if not impossible, to measure. When selecting a service provider, customers take a leap of faith in making their choice. Successful product brands are often identified with physical marks or symbols, but creating similar icons for services requires a degree of translation (in the mind of the customer) once these icons are removed from the actual offer. Thus, good branding and brand communications are vital to success.

Most services companies use success stories and track records to demonstrate their capabilities, wherever and whenever they can. With the advent of many new technologies, however, this is sometimes difficult to do. Thus, a good brand reputation helps a great deal. Many companies in the business of providing solutions for clients use "prototyping" (mock-up of solutions) technology and techniques to better manage communications barriers and expectations. These in themselves can be very time- and resource-consuming. No matter how synthetically good they may appear, their impact on the client will be tempered by the brand image of the service provider in terms of reputation or customer experience.

Managing comparisons

The hi-tech service market is relatively new. This fact and its intangible character explain why there is little benchmark information or objective third-party evaluation. Its implications for hi-tech service companies are twofold. The first is the difficulty of convincing clients that one's company is different and better than the rest. (This positioning problem is discussed in Chapter 4.) The other, and related to the first, is the issue of the "value" of the brand itself. Most research companies that try to evaluate service-based technology brands base their findings on different dimensions and niches that may not provide consistent comparisons. For example, a service company that commands US$1,000 in daily per capita rates may not necessarily possess more brand value than that which commands only US$500 each day. That value may depend on the total man-effort required to deliver a total solution on the initial cost or life cycle cost, or on the organizational support costs required to support the manpower effort.

IBM, Microsoft, Intel, and HP have been ranked as some of the world's most valuable hi-tech brands. But these are all hi-tech product (software and hardware) companies. It would be interesting to know the brand value of IT service companies such as Computer Science Company, EDS, PriceWaterhouseCoopers, KPMG, Andersen Consulting, Arthur Andersen, and Ernst & Young. As yet, they do not appear to have been valued. (Chapter 8 talks about brand valuation in detail.)

Managing client expectations

As services are much harder to standardize than products, service buyers normally do not see the final output before the purchase. The purchase decision is based on agreed specifications that buyers and sellers may interpret differently. In mission-critical applications, the selection of a service provider to support, say, an investment or Internet banking operation, may be a "bet-the-company" decision to some firms. In other words, the investment may be so important that the whole survival of the company might depend on the risk element of choosing the service provider. This decision may be made more difficult by the fact that the buyers may have no idea what is a realistic expectation concerning the service provider's offerings. The purchase decision for hi-tech services thus becomes a brand decision on which brand can be trusted. Branding therefore pays off.

Understanding the decision maker is also vital to managing client expectations. Decision makers in client companies generally base their purchase decisions on a service provider's ability to deliver quality service on time, instead of on technology features, which are mostly similar. In the past, a chief information officer (CIO) would not be blamed for service delivery failures if he chose the services of a popular brand like IBM. On the contrary, the same CIO might have to justify his decision if other "color" vendors were deemed or proven to have better solutions. This is because most CIOs or IT managers may be just as concerned with how the purchase decision will reflect on them as they are with the technical strengths or weaknesses of the service provider's offering. Again, branding counts.

The development and design of a hi-tech service brand thus relies heavily on an accurate analysis of the target audience. In most cases, technology service decisions are made by informed committees that deliberate for months on the "virtual" or "intangible" product intended to be purchased. In addition, the people involved in purchase decisions may weigh various performance factors differently. But brands transcend all that. When everything appears equal, the brand becomes the decisive factor.

Managing multiple partnerships and co-branding

Most service providers offer one-stop services to their customers, requiring them to manage the entire networks of value-adding partners, ranging from consulting firms to systems integrators, from independent software vendors to resellers, and from hardware manufacturers to distributors. The brand positioning of a small service provider may depend on the brand positioning of its product partners, which are in most cases big global brand names. In such cases, it will not be easy for a smaller service provider to establish its own brand personality or character. But if the smaller company works hard on its branding, then attracting the right partners becomes less of a problem.

In fact, one of the objectives of developing and perpetuating a strong and recognizable brand is to attract partners. Seeking partners for services is undertaken for two main reasons: to break into new markets and to help establish credibility. As potential partner targets are considered, two of the characteristics that are closely evaluated are the organizations' strengths in marketing and sales, and their "brand pull."

Starbucks is a good example. It is not a hi-tech company but uses a hi-tech strategy, and has in fact attracted hi-tech partners. Starbucks has made investments in Living.com and TalkCity, but its ability to attract hi-tech companies is an investment in itself. Moreover, the delivery service company Kozmo.com is reportedly paying Starbucks US$150 million over five years to advertise in its outlets, where it has installed boxes for video tapes rented from Kozmo—a good example of brand power, and how hi-tech and non-hi-tech companies can work together. Were it not for its brand name, Starbucks would not be given e-business opportunities.

Another example is the recent tie-up between Virgin and SingTel to create Virgin Mobile, a US$1-billion start-up business that aims to market mobile phone products in Asia. SingTel understands the Asian info-communications market, but Virgin has a powerful brand name that is not just the most well-known brand name in the U.K., but is also known the world over. The fit would appear to be very good, especially if aimed at the younger market where Virgin excels.

Much of the debate around the negotiating table centers on how the partners will co-brand. The power brands need to carefully monitor the use of their names and marks by developing design guidelines and communicating copyright restrictions. More importantly, they must decide when the proliferation of their brand crosses the line from increased exposure to confusion and dilution.

Managing customer relationships

In technology services, companies have to market the brand experience via multiple dimensions, not just price and performance. That means investing in relationship-building activities across the promotional mix. Besides being educational, these require meeting the customers face to face. They include customer conferences, technology exhibitions, seminars, CEO breakfast meetings, leadership forums, visits to expertise centers, and trade shows. NCS, for instance, regularly invites its customers to cultural events, movies, museum visits, and sporting events. It also sponsors client activities such as sports.

These kinds of initiatives often prove successful in building customer relationships, unlike traditional advertising and marketing methods. For example, traditional direct marketing techniques that have proven to be reasonably successful in selling products fail miserably in building relationships. Real brand value is at the heart of strong relationships with customers. And value need not be defined narrowly in terms of features and performance. Value in hi-tech service markets, as in other markets, is a much more complex concept, and is related to overall service satisfaction.

Managing service quality

All power brands deliver quality products and services. Quality is therefore one thing that hi-tech service companies must concentrate on all the time. It may not bring differentiation, but it is the price to pay to gain market entry. In this light, what do customers look for in hi-tech services?

In a customer survey carried out in January 2000, NCS customers ranked the following service qualities in order of importance:

- reliability (dependable round the clock, seven days a week)
- solutions quality (which meets their needs and creates business value)
- responsiveness (excellent help desk and support)
- assurance (knowledgeable, and conveys trust and confidence)
- partnership (a win-win long-term relationship)
- empathy (for the problems, deadlines, and other difficulties clients must face)
- value for money (not just a matter of cost, but the value obtained in terms of quality, reliability)
- presentation (by the services company in its materials, communications)

Companies in hi-tech services wanting to establish strong brands and a good reputation would do well to focus on all of these aspects of quality. To do otherwise is to court failure.

Building the brand culture

Services are really all about people—human attributes, values, characteristics, and shared experiences. Product branding often attempts to assign personality characteristics to the brand, usually fuelled by a massive amount of advertising on the part of the seller. It takes a great deal of time and money to ensure that product brands gain not just the rational but the vital emotional support essential for consumer acceptance and loyalty.

Service companies, however, have a built-in advantage in that they can, if they motivate and train their employees well, demonstrate brand personality much more easily. They can be reliable, responsive, friendly, smart, flexible, cool, innovative, and even fun. In this respect, branding is not the sole function of corporate marketing. It is a human resource commitment too, as brands must be brought to life by everyone in the company. For service brands, the way to do this is by explaining the brand personality to the employees, and helping them apply the characteristics to their everyday work. Training and development can also play a much greater role in establishing the brand personality by involving the staff in the entire process of hi-tech brand development.

Branding and change management

If branding is all about managing perceptions and good value propositions, then it is important to ensure that what consumers expect matches what they receive. Not only must external communications tie in closely with what the company can offer and how it is offered, staff in a service company must know the value propositions and be fully committed to delivering on the promises. This means that everyone has to be clear about their role, and what the company should and could do to ensure customer delight. This in turn means that any technology service company must have a good change management system in operation to keep up with the changing demands of the hi-tech marketplace.

For example, NCS formed taskforces to identify the needs of customers and to develop integrated plans that would ensure that everyone in the organization was able to live up to the brand promise.

The company also embarked on a massive change program to get the staff's commitment and to ensure that they understood the key messages intended for the marketplace and the company's expectations of them. To ensure mass support at the ground level, the company engaged the staff from each site and unit in the change process. Role models, chosen as change agents, served as the link between management and staff. They attended workshops to develop skills as communicators and facilitators. They in turn conducted mini-sessions to get feedback and monitor the progress of the program.

There were also road shows to explain change management and key branding messages. When staff understood the messages, the external campaigns started. Change program workshops became a part of the core training program for all staff, while special emphasis was given to the development of soft skills, including the projection of a professional image, communication, and presentation techniques. The change program has had various phases and is still ongoing today. In the hi-tech world, change is a constant, and so change training has to be so too, moving people from an awareness level to an action level, and from habits to core values, and helping them acquire such skills as flexibility and adaptability.

When communication campaigns are underway, staff are informed of their rationale and encouraged to gather feedback from customers. This generates excitement, as employees become rapidly interested in the brand and the management of the brand image. In NCS's case, most of the staff gave constructive comments that were used to fine-tune the creative aspects of the campaigns. Several discussions and activities then started in a "Think Tank" in the intranet. The Think Tank is an intranet-based discussion bulletin board where staff can post suggestions online, and give their inputs to other ideas put forward. It serves as a very good repository site, too.

Managing brand communication

The other challenge facing companies involved in hi-tech services branding is the ability to cut through the clutter created by multimedia blitzes, and not simply add to the noise already bombarding the buyers. This is a function both of money and method. With the exception of hi-tech services targeting consumer markets such as those for mobile phones, PCs, and smart card services, many technology service brands cannot compete with the big fast-moving consumer goods spenders, such as Procter & Gamble, in the airwaves. Service marketing budgets are still a fraction of the sum being spent on IT products. Therefore, service providers have to be very clever about both the message and the method chosen to communicate that message.

Perhaps the most significant factor in determining communications investments is that the buyers of IT services are a relatively targeted audience that does not require advertisements through such media as television and newspapers, which have a massive reach.

Much has been written about the role of advertising in building strong brands, but for hi-tech service companies it is seldom the right approach. Some image- and product-related advertising can be carried out, but for the vast majority of these companies that do not have the size or the resources of the traditional hi-tech firms such as IBM, it is more important to have a focused, cost-effective communications strategy. This includes managing media relationships well, creating good public relations, and getting involved in the right kind of sponsorship and events. Here are some examples of the kind of activities that work, based on the experience of NCS.

- *Public relations in branding hi-tech services*
  As NCS has found out, public relations (PR) is important to service companies, especially in their early years. NCS realized that PR was the only powerful communications weapon that could really have an impact on the marketplace in the first three years of its operation after it was privatized. For a young company, every significant achievement counts, and therefore it must be made known. Brand communication then becomes a story after story of successful implementation, and an announcement after announcement of partnerships. The criteria for announcements are not that critical,

but informing people about the company's achievements is. So, for smaller companies this tack is a good use of limited communications resources.

NCS used PR to launch a branding campaign. The lead media was also print, and the theme was kept simple and bold—namely, that NCS was Singapore's best-kept secret and the architect of the Singapore Civil Service Computerization program.

As a result of the campaign, existing customers felt reassured, potential customers took note, and staff pride went up. These improvements were tracked through internal and external surveys, and advertisement acceptance surveys. At this stage the correlation between a favorable image and customer satisfaction became evident. As with the branding of products, companies should remember that it is not possible to create a powerful brand image without giving customers top quality.

- *Events, sponsorships, and similar activities*
  Hi-tech service companies have to be very focused in their external marketing activities. NCS ensured that any corporate-driven events were aimed at CEOs/CIOs/CFOs, and that any above-the-line programs utilized channels preferred by these elite groups, such as the high-profile regional publications like *Newsweek*, *Fortune*, *Asiaweek*, and *BusinessWeek*. These powerful brands not only reach the right target audiences, they also give advertisers credibility.

  Events and seminars are very good networking opportunities that reinforce leadership in the industry. Companies can build their reputation over time by organizing quality events. An even more effective approach is co-branding with a renowned entity. In line with this, NCS tied up with *Fortune* to organize the NCS-Fortune Leaders series. This was a smart approach because *Fortune* was considered an excellent partner in ensuring the success of the event. Delegates also had the confidence that they would have a fruitful time at the event.

Aside from co-branding with key customers and top players, NCS also extended its presence to the local community by supporting local initiatives like theater productions and challenges like the Antarctica 2000 expedition. NCS also further boosted its reputation by accumulating awards and public recognition. Among these are the IT Person of the Year awards for its leaders and the distinct honor of having the highest number of IT project managers certified in Singapore.

Regardless of which strategies they adopt, hi-tech service companies have to be very clear about their target audiences. If companies carry products and services, then it is important to reach out to both the users and the key decision makers. In most cases, they should direct their messages to the latter, particularly the CEOs and top managers, who often decide on matters involving massive and long-term investments in IT. For them, there is a real need to ensure success with a reputable company, and there is a minimum comfort level that must be established.

PR and other non-advertising activities represent more value for the marketing budget, and can be very powerful for growing hi-tech service companies. For hi-tech branding, frequency is not as important as the quality of communication. A few major scoops are worth much more than frequent but negligible messages. Remember that it is a noisy world out there. So, stand out once in a while and over time, and your target audiences will perceive a regular rhythm. A sustained effort is therefore very crucial.

Service branding benefits

The following are the eight common benefits hi-tech service companies gain when they invest in branding:

1. *Get into the shortlist of targeted prospects and achieve market momentum.* While government and government agencies generally provide equal opportunities for all to bid for projects, commercial companies look for trusted partners. High mind share

(through brand awareness) increases the chances of being contacted first for new opportunities.

2. *Evolve from a cost-based to a value-based proposition.* Customers are willing to pay for well-known brand names. For example, Andersen Consulting is able to charge its clients multiples of the fee charges of local hi-tech consultancy service companies, even though all may have similarly experienced consultants.

3. *Recruit talent and attract partners.* Strongly branded companies are attractive to people who are looking for jobs and businesses looking for strategic partners. Brands are like magnets in that they attract people, but more than this, they motivate them too.

4. *Value-add to market positioning.* Strong brand names add vitality and trust to client relationships, making the customer's decision making easier when considering which service company to employ. The brand itself becomes the differentiator.

5. *Increase shareholder value.* The somewhat high costs of branding companies, in terms of advertising and promotion expenditure, are more than recouped by the premium prices gained, and the increased market capitalization over and above relatively unbranded companies.

6. *Create competitive entry barriers.* A strong brand is a competitive advantage in itself. As you will read in Chapter 8, Boeing and McDonnell Douglas created such high entry barriers that several European countries were forced to form strong alliances to produce Airbus, which would compete in the North American and global markets. As in product markets like these, many hi-tech service companies now have to identify niche areas to dominate, as opposed to competing head-on with, reputable brands that already have an established market share.

7. *Enhance customer relationships and trust.* A reputable brand is an icon of trustworthiness and confidence for customers. This is especially important to service-oriented companies that market intangibles. A commercially recognized brand increases the initial trust level.

8. *Shorten the sales cycle.* With a strong brand name behind them, sales persons of companies can focus their energy and sales expenditure on marketing their service solutions, instead of spending time trying to get noticed. Brand recognition and a good brand image allow them to enter straight away into the second level of sales. This shortens the sales cycle and reduces sales costs.

In sum, creating a strong brand image for hi-tech service companies is not without its challenges, but the benefits are great. Planned well, it will bring in innumerable benefits, as were pointed out in this chapter. Done haphazardly, it could prove to be a total waste of time, effort, and money. The case study below illustrates how changing brand messages can turn confidence into confusion.

CASE STUDY
MERRILL LYNCH
Making radical changes to a staid corporate brand image

In an effort to address its rather staid corporate brand image and show people that it is an integral part of the modern hi-tech world, Merrill Lynch has re-engineered its icon—the bull—and embarked on a major advertising campaign that coincides with its entry into online trading. The company has introduced low-cost online investing for customers, and has had to break away from its traditional brokerage image, especially as it has lost out to successful online brokerages such as Charles Schwab Corp. and E*Trade Group Inc. Some of the new commercials show real-life customers describing how profitable their relationship with the company has been, while other advertisements show the Merrill Lynch bull icon in a digitalized wired-up format. While the bull remains a symbol of the power and durability of the Merrill Lynch brand, the jazzy new hi-tech bull signifies readiness to fight in the e-commerce market arena. One two-page newspaper advertisement released early this year showed the new bull with the following copy:

"Be quick.
Be smart.
Be ready.
Be prudent.
Be daring.
Be conventional.
Be contrarian.
Be global.
Be local.
Be backward-looking.
Be forward-looking.
Be strategic.
Be wired.
Be unwired.
Be thoughtful.
Be spontaneous.
Be wise.

Be bullish."

The contradictions and the "everything to everyone" nature of this copy may well suggest that the company does not know how it really wants to be seen. Some critics of the commercials said that the customers profiled appeared anything but confident about the firm's new offerings, with some looking confused. Time will tell whether perceptions of the brand image have changed. It does appear, however, that Merrill Lynch may not have done enough to convince the public that it has what it takes to be a major player in the digital world.

By contrast, advertisements run a few months earlier were much stronger and more focused, carrying much clearer emotional messages— for example:

"If you want to see something
Done, just tell some human beings

It can't be done. Make it known that
It's impossible to fly to the moon,
Or run a hundred meters in nine-
Point-nine seconds, or solve Fermat's
Last Theorem. Remind the world that
No one has ever hit sixty-two home
Runs in a season. Stuffed eighteen
People into a Volkswagen Bug. Set
half the world free. Or cloned a sheep.
Dangle the undoable in front of
the world. Then, consider it done."

The tag line was "Human Achievement" with the Merrill Lynch name and the original bull icon. To us, these messages were powerful and relevant. The new messages present a brand personality that is somewhat schizophrenic, and their meaning is not clear at all.

Whether advertising agencies are changed or not, companies should think very hard before making radical changes to their brand identity and communications. Update the brand, yes, but keep the messages clear and consistent.

8

Future Hi-Tech
Branding Perspectives

It is difficult to say exactly what is going to happen to technology businesses in the future, particularly those that are Internet-based. We can only point to emerging trends. The two most important of these relate to size, specifically the trend toward mergers and acquisitions, and the trend toward measuring brand value. It is unlikely that these two will go away. In fact, they are likely to become increasingly important in the hi-tech business's pursuit of success.

THE WORLD OF MERGERS, ACQUISITIONS, AND ALLIANCES

Small is beautiful but big is better

The paradox of size is with us. While being small seems to be a necessary element of speed and flexibility, the thirst for customer critical mass drives the trend toward bigger size. In the physical hi-tech business world, where investment in technology is by necessity huge, size drives down costs and secures efficiency. In the virtual business world, small companies can maneuver faster than their larger competitors in niche markets, and the struggle to get big enough to attack global markets is not so much a problem. Electronic commerce has removed the necessity for large distribution channels, for example. But when small Internet businesses want to capitalize on their brand names and move into broader markets, as Amazon.com has done, then again size becomes important, because they have to reach a critical mass of customers to make the strategies work. Thus, one very evident trend in the hi-tech world is the tendency of size to be a dominant part of corporate planning.

Mergers, acquisitions, and alliances (MA&A)

In 1999 the value of reported mergers and acquisitions (M&A) exceeded US$3,195 billion worldwide. The trend is accelerating, and the wave of M&A alliances and joint venture (JV) activities is transforming whole industries. Examples of M&A activity abound, such as those of Virgin Atlantic and Singapore Airlines, AOL and Time Warner, CSA & CSC, Vodafone and Mannesmann, and more. In Europe, for instance, mergers have accelerated among its telecommunications carriers, and many involve enormous vendors, such as the merger between Telecom Italia and Olivetti, and the one between Telia and Telenor.

One catalyst for this trend is deregulation, which in many of the world's markets has created intense competition and overcapacity. The pressure is on for companies to protect or increase their market share and simultaneously cut costs to stay competitive. The large brands are driving down costs and investing in marketing to drive out higher cost-based, undifferentiated competitors. And niche brands have to defend their markets rigorously. Those that fail to do so are taken over by larger brands that seek market know-how, capacity and, above all, the brands themselves. In all companies the issue being discussed is which brands to buy, support, develop or withdraw.

The automotive industry also provides instances of global MA&A activity. Examples are the US$33-billion Daimler–Chrysler merger in 1999, and Ford's takeover of Volvo's car division for US$6.4 billion in January 1999. The brand acquisition process at work here is also evident in many other industries.

A further reason for the trend toward size is brand power itself. A strong brand facilitates the establishment of joint ventures and the formation of strategic alliances. A good example is the strategic alliance formed by Singapore Airlines, Delta, and Swiss Air, which effectively increases the overall value of all three airlines. Alliances are also increasing in an effort to make the sales numbers and have a global presence, as typified by the Star Alliance of 14 airlines. Increasingly, acquisitions and alliances are being driven by the objective of "capturing" more customers to ensure a revenue stream, or to expand the market within which new products and services can be delivered. This facilitates cross-selling of brands. Most companies find that sitting in their local market and defending it against predatory attack is not the way to go. The way to go is to go out into international markets to establish a wider customer base. This is no easy task, but alliances with similar companies intent on doing the same, or buying other brands, can help make it possible.

Strong alliances can also create unbeatable energy and market strength. Airbus is a case in point. In the 1970 and 1980s, Boeing and McDonnell Douglas dominated the market for large commercial aircraft. To protect their home markets, the French, German, Dutch, Belgian, British, and Spanish aircraft companies joined forces to build a commercial aircraft that would rival that of the American giants. After some initial hiccups, the European consortium began to pose a serious threat to Boeing and McDonnell Douglas. For example, in June 1992, Airbus succeeded in filling 30% of new orders for commercial aircraft, and is now on the order list of most large airlines in the world. Moreover, it has penetrated the North American home market of the two former market leaders. It did so by offering leading-edge technology and a full complement of aircraft and, more significantly, by capitalizing on the brand image and strength of the alliance. Airbus has become a model for many companies that increasingly consider forming alliances to produce products that they cannot manage or develop if they operate individually. The joining together of several companies to create a new brand ideally suits such mega-project and high-risk ventures.

As new market developments emerge, so do company alliances to exploit their potential. For example, IBM, i2 Technologies, and Ariba formed an alliance in March 2000 to capture market share in the online marketplace business that linked companies and their suppliers. At least 800 of these marketplaces now exist, and they allow firms to gain substantial cost efficiencies through online links to many suppliers. In this triumverate, IBM supplies the hardware, transaction software, services, and database, i2 the software that facilitates purchase and delivery coordination, and Ariba the software that automates online transactions.

The three organizations have created a US90-million advertising campaign to position the partnership as the leading operator of Internet commerce marketplaces using the catchphrases "What a great location for an e-marketplace" and "it's b2bx3." The advertisements are intended to appear in European and Asian countries. For IBM this is just a part of its massive drive to own "e-business," the word it invented, as it is already spending US$660 million a year on e-business advertising.

Important MA&A brand considerations

a) Brand equity

One of the most common issues in an alliance scenario is brand equity. It is now common for companies to undertake brand due diligence before and after acquisition to ensure that they make correct decisions regarding the maintenance and development of specific brands. As BMW's acquisition of Rover demonstrates, the risk to shareholder value of getting such value studies wrong is huge. BMW had to pump money into Rover without any gains in profits, and recently had to let go of the company for a token sum, assuming most of the debts as part of the deal.

b) Brand positioning

Determining how the new company or partnership will be marketed and identified to customers and suppliers is another strategic issue that must be addressed throughout the M&A transaction. Daimler-Benz and Chrysler opted to keep the two brands entirely separate to avoid customer confusion and keep brand loyalty.

In the case of AOL and Time Warner, they made history in the last decade by setting a record price for the merger of the two organizations.

But what will happen to the positioning of both brands? Will one be dropped in favor of the other? This mega-merger will continue to be closely watched by industry observers.

If the key impetus toward the partnership is to strengthen product offerings, protect existing market share, and enhance efficiency in operations, then it may be more efficient for both brands to remain independent and market themselves separately. Indeed, both are at different levels in the product supply chain—one in access and the other in content. Each could be positioned differently to best suit its own key markets.

c) Brand localization

Cultures vary across the world, and what may appeal to one culture may not elicit similar responses in another. It is therefore very important that brand managers understand what makes different country audiences tick and what may offend their sensibilities. In this respect, the success of a product or service depends on the localization of its contents to appeal to its new audience. The adage "think global, act local" still has validity.

If a product needs to be created from scratch or if customizing a product is going to succeed, one can increase its chances of success by leveraging on a global brand. This leapfrogs the need to create awareness and allows a company to get straight to work on the acceptance level. A good example of this is top cyberbrand Lycos, which successfully reached out to a new market across geographic regions.

In the search and content game, speed of retrieval and relevance are important. It is likewise essential to establish a strong local presence in the markets targeted—and at Internet speed. But when it comes to creating brand awareness, there are no differences between technology products and traditional goods. Hi-tech businesses still need to create awareness to drive people to their product, in this case, the Web site. They must also make sure that the position of the brand and the messages are sensitive to the local environment.

In Lycos's case, it had a problem extending and leveraging the single brand name into Asia, because a spanner in the form of cybersquatters was thrown into the works. Cybersquatters are Internet bandits that pre-register any brand names hoping to sell them for large sums of money. Lycos was faced with this problem when it tried to move into Asia. Thus, it had to develop a transition name until the preferred names were either negotiated or returned by law. As URLs like www.lycos.com.sg and www.lycos.com.my (for Singapore and Malaysia, respectively) had been taken up and would not be available until a year or two later, a new entity, LycosAsia, was created. Though not as efficient as promoting on a single entity, this is a smart brand extension as it is still leveraging on the master Lycos name. And LycosAsia completed the localization process by providing a high level of local content in all of the countries it operates in.

d) Brands within brands

Every technology product is a complex system made up of subsystems, each of which is developed and manufactured by a different industry. Take the computer, for example. Its components involve the semiconductor industry, disk drive industry with brand names such as Seagate; the peripherals industry with brand names such as HP, Epson, Canon printers; power suppliers; monitor manufacturers; and the software industry, just to mention a few.

Branding issues get more complicated for the computer manufacturer. When Intel decided to spend US$500 million a year on the now famous "Intel Inside" campaign, PC manufacturers such as Sony and Compaq had to consider whether to use as well the Intel logo in their advertisements. This posed some difficulty to Compaq, which acquired Digital, a direct competitor of Intel. However, in most cases, brands can co-exist in harmony and end up supporting each other.

e) Co-branding or brand partnerships

When new features are a constant, a bigger customer base is essential, and speed to market is vital, it often makes sense to co-brand. Co-branding allows two or more brands to leverage off the strength of each other. Co-branding enables cross-selling and faster penetration into targeted markets. It also reduces marketing costs, which are shared. Manchester United is a world-famous club, with fans and members from all ages and walks of life. Through its club membership card, supporters enjoy privileges offered by numerous merchants and retailers around the world. By tying up with other card bases, such as Singapore's Never Ending Wishes (NEW) loyalty card, Manchester United got the opportunity to ride on NEW's existing merchant network and its underlying back-end infrastructure to process payment, track activities, and create comprehensive databases of its customers. With a stroke, both brands created a bigger playing field and brought more value to their users. For NEW, more merchants and co-brand partners mean more demand and acceptance of its infrastructure services. With more support and funding, it has been able to enhance the existing system, thus widening the entry barriers for similar services—capabilities that others would find difficult to duplicate due to heavy capital and upfront investment.

f) *Partnerships build brands quickly*

Technology allows companies to explore partnerships and alliances in ways that are difficult using traditional marketing methods. Amazon.com is able to implement its Associates Program with other technology leaders such as America Online, Yahoo, Netscape, and the @Home Network. Through these partnerships, consumers are invited into the world of Amazon.com, almost like a referral from a friend. Even these kinds of relationships among brands, commonplace in technology, create different dynamics from a brand that is a stand-alone and that is tightly controlled by the manufacturer. Yet, while companies diffuse the brand and co-mingle it with other brands, these relationships create a stronger, interrelated brand network for the consumer. The secret is to give your brand the desired exposure necessary on the Internet environment without being eclipsed by partner brands.

g) *Looking for brand and culture compatibility*

Brand and culture compatibility are definitely a major ingredient in successful co-branding and alliances. In co-branding, your existing customer base would now have to accept another set of values that the co-brand brings. If it fits, the cross-selling process can bring great results. If the brand values are incompatible, customers might be turned off. Likewise for alliances, buyers of one brand may be forced to experience the services offered by the allied parties. If the standards are not compatible, this could mean the end of a relationship.

Branding and culture compatibility need not necessarily be a problem when the services provided are distinct. An example is an upward or downward integration in a supply chain, where it is possible for each organization to have its own brand and culture. Acquisition in this scenario could bring added savings, as each organization does not have to pay a premium for services if it controls the upstream or downstream operations.

h) *Brand transfer*

With the degree of industry consolidation at an all-time high—and with no sign of stabilization in sight—the impact on established brands is of great concern to integration teams. Possibly one of the more difficult decisions associated with mergers and acquisitions, for example, is how to position the new combined value proposition, as mentioned above. In some cases the choice is clear—retain the power brand and dissolve the others. But what about a wholly-owned subsidiary? And what about the sub-branding of divisions? From a branding point of view, the only bad decision is the creation of a hybrid, which amounts to a lack of decision or a poor compromise.

Apple is a unique example of brand transfer that was not an offshoot of acquisition. Though at its lowest point in 1996–97 when it was in the red, Apple still enjoyed considerable brand loyalty from a devoted group of followers for whom that brand was synonymous with the Apple's simplicity and its utility for their particular needs. Apple successfully created Macintosh. The younger generation today is associated more with Macintosh, while the iMac has enjoyed enormous popularity, the result of Steve Jobs's thus-far-successful efforts to refocus the company's marketing and product development strategies.

Brand naming dilemmas

Whenever major mergers and acquisitions transpose, the firms involved are clearly concerned about two major issues affecting brand loyalty—namely, the new company name for the merged entity, and what to do with the brands under the new company.

Citibank and Travellers Group, for instance, merely combined their names to form Citigroup. But Daimler Benz and Chrysler, while combining the names to form DaimlerChrysler, had a great deal of discussion about how and where their respective brands would be communicated and sold. The decision was that none of each company's brands would be sold off the same premises. As far as brand communications is concerned, there is little change. So, while they are all set to reap the economies of scale as far as operations are concerned, those achievable through combined advertising and promotions activities have been sacrificed to preclude customer confusion and brand cannibalization.

Exxon and Mobil were equally decisive about their brand dilemma when they merged to form an organization with combined sales of US$147 billion. They showed great concern about the possible effects on consumers of combining names and the need for transparency in what they were doing. As a result, the new Exxon Mobil Corporation came out with an advertisement in December 1999 that read:

"We're as brand loyal as you are."
Loyalty is a two-way street. So along the street, road, or motorway we aren't about to confuse our customers. Yes, we've merged. But our brands Esso, Mobil, and Exxon will still be there. What will change is the company behind them. ExxonMobil is a new name for technology, efficiency, and service. Helping our old names treat you better than ever."

The ad, which carried the Web site address www.exxon.mobil.com, showed the two organizations' respective brand logos, with the company sign-off ExxonMobil. It is interesting to note that the advertisement promises a new and better experience for its consumers. Whether this is deliverable in a short span of time remains to be seen.

TotalFina did not make such quick decisions on brands following its takeover of Elf Aquitaine, but considered three scenarios. The first of these was to gain marketing synergies by converting all brands to the Total name; a second was to create a new global brand name; and the third was to allow the existing brands to continue as they were before the merger. As this book was being written, the three options were still under consideration. The problem is that Total and Fina are still operating largely as distinctive brands in many countries and are likely to continue to do so. Whatever the outcome, any re-branding is likely to be a costly activity.

And to see just how costly re-branding can be, and how companies at times look from the inside out rather than take an outside-in approach, consider the BP Amoco initiative.

Shortly after becoming the world's third largest publicly listed oil group with a market value of US$200 billion, BP Amoco undertook a rebranding exercise. Bringing together British Petroleum, Amoco Corporation, Atlantic Richfield, and Burmah Castrol into one strong identity is a mammoth task, and will take years to complete. The "BP" will remain, cashing in on the previous equity of one of the group, but the initials will now stand for "beyond petroleum."

Chief executive John Brown said, "We have adopted a single brand to show our customers around the world that, wherever they see the BP sign, they can consistently expect the highest quality of products and services. Pre-brand research and preparation evidently cost around US$7 million, and another US$200 million is expected to be spent on brand support and advertising." Brown also said that he was sure that the new brand would "greatly strengthen the sense of identity and common purpose of our 100,000 staff."

A typical double-page spread explaining the move on the launch of the new brand to the public reads:

"BP, Amoco, ARCO, Castrol.

What does it add up to?

It means a new company able to offer global energy solutions.

It means a company that makes petrol and diesel that produce lower emissions.

It means the world's leading producer of solar power.

It means the talent and resources to go beyond what people expect. Today, 100,000 employees in 100 countries join together to form a new company called BP. Tomorrow, we begin building a new brand of progress for the world."

The text almost reads as though the new company is trying to convince itself that it has made a good move. At best it describes what it can do and its corporate strength; at worst it displays a self-centred and somewhat arrogant brand personality. The consumer response is likely to be, "So what?" Quite a lot of money for a weak consumer value proposition, don't you think?

In general, the rule of brand naming is that once you have a strong brand name, never change it, if it can be helped. The BP example shows some respect for this rule. The company probably found in its research, just as others have, that established brand names have a great deal of brand equity locked up in them in the form of strong emotional associations and loyalty, and that changing brand names can lead to unhappy customers and a loss of business. But while the BP companies tried to salvage some brand equity from the merged entities, the naming rule did not seem to deter Rhone-Poulenc and Hoechst, two well-known brand names that, on merging, created a totally new and relatively meaningless name, Aventis. Huge amounts of money will have to be spent on merely gaining brand awareness for the new entity, not to mention the tremendous loss of equity that has been destroyed by the removal of well-known and trusted brand names.

The point to note about these examples is that brands are powerful entities in their own right, and people get deeply attached to them.

Careful consideration has to be given to creating new brand names, or combining brand names, which could result in brand clashes that may destroy the valuable equity in terms of both loyalty and asset value that have been built over a substantial period of time.

THE BRAND AS A STRATEGIC ASSET— BRAND VALUATION

Brands are intangible assets. That they are intangible has, until recently, been a thorn in the side of those wishing to leverage the value of powerful companies that own little. Now the true value of brands can be measured and leveraged.

One issue on everybody's lips today is the value of brands. Some people talk about *brand equity* and some *brand value*. However these terms are used, what people are really interested in is what a company is worth. These people may either be investors, analysts, owners, employees with profit shares and/or stock options, media, or other individuals interested in the company. And as the worth of the brand can be multiples of the net assets of a company, ultimately it is the financial worth of a brand that is meaningful to companies, whether they are hi-tech or not. Studies show, however, that the full value of brand-owning companies is not explicitly shown in many accounts, and that the bulk of intangible asset value remains "off balance sheet." A study conducted by Brand Finance Plc, for instance, indicated that for 344 of the FTSE 350 companies with year-ends up to and including December 31, 1998, 72% of the value of those companies was not reflected in published balance sheets. Brands form a significant part of this unexplained value.

For hi-tech companies, the brand is becoming more and more important for reasons mentioned earlier in the book. Indeed, for Net-based technology companies, the brand appears to be the lifeline for survival, as the fundamentals of many companies do not justify the share price. In some cases, larger losses appear to lead to larger market capitalization! What is happening is that investors are, to all intents and purposes, buying the brands. The high valuation of Internet brands reflects market opinion that the early brand leaders will clean up as the market matures. Brand valuation will become more important as a marketing discipline for these and any companies that take branding seriously, particularly now that robust methodologies are available to set the standards for determining brand worth.

Brand value methodology

"Economic use" valuations are the most popular approach to valuing brands. They consider the owner's returns on his investment as the result of owning the brand—that is, the brand's net contribution to the business, both now and in the future. These valuations draw on internal information, supported by market research. They do not consider the value of the brand in use by a different owner or any "hope" value based on new uses of the brand. What we really want to know, however, is the value of future earnings stemming from the brand's pact with its consumers. So, it is becoming more common for economic-use valuations to be based on the discounted value of future brand earnings. Typically, such brand valuations contain four elements, namely:

a) a financial analysis (to identify branded business earnings)

b) a branded analysis (to determine what proportion of business earnings are attributable to the brand)

c) a brand risk analysis (to assess the security of the brand franchise, both with customers and with end consumers)

d) a legal analysis (to establish that the brand is a true piece of "property")

Uses of brand valuation

In the last few years, brand valuation has become an accepted technique in a wide range of applications, especially the following:

- MA&As: Brand valuation plays a major part in the planning of these undertakings. Potential acquirers of branded goods companies, and their investors and bankers, find comfort in the knowledge that the price being paid for a company can be substantiated by reference to the value of the specific intangible, as well as tangible, assets being acquired.

- *External investor relations*: Some major companies say that building a portfolio of world-class brands is a central objective. Brand valuation can be used to provide hard numbers in support of what is otherwise a soft argument.
- *Internal communications*: Brand valuation can help to explain performance and be used as a means of motivating management. The use of internal royalty rates based on brand values can also make it clear to a group of companies the value of the corporate assets they are being allowed to use.
- *Marketing budget allocation*: Brand valuation can assist in budgeting decisions, providing a more systematic basis for decision making.
- *Internal marketing management*: Strategic use of brand valuation techniques allows senior management to compare the success of different brand strategies and the relative performance of particular marketing teams.
- *Balance sheet reporting*: In certain parts of the world, acquired brands are now carried as intangible assets and amortized.
- *Licensing and franchising*: Accurate brand valuation allows a realistic set of charges to be created for the licensing and franchising of brand names.
- *Securitized borrowing*: Companies such as Disney and Levi Strauss have borrowed major sums against their brand names.
- *Litigation support*: Brand valuations have been used in legal cases to defend the brand value, such as the illicit use of a brand name or receivership.
- *Fair trading investigations*: Brand valuation has been used to explain to non-marketing audiences the role of brands and the importance their value has for the companies that spend so much to acquire and maintain them.
- *Tax planning*: More and more companies are actively planning the most effective domicile for their brand portfolios with branded royalty streams in mind.

- *New product and market development assessment*: New business strategies can be modeled using brand valuation techniques to make judgments on, for example, the best brand, best market extension, and best consumer segment.

Hi-tech companies are already using brand valuation in an effort to gain maximum advantage from their brand names, as explained below.

Traditional versus Internet brands

Many traditional brands are lagging behind the Internet brands; they appear to be slow to respond to the Internet challenge. THINK New Idea's Fortune 500 1999 survey revealed that although 90% of Fortune 500 companies had an Internet site, only 10% allowed a two-way interaction to include feedback, suggestions, and chatrooms, while only 4% had e-commerce transactions capability. If traditional brands do not shape up, they will be left behind. They must overcome the problems of channel conflicts and price differentials that they face with online and offline retail strategies. In the future, because of these problems, we will see many traditional brand companies creating totally new brands for Internet offerings, such as Egg, Marbles, and Smile in the financial services industry.

Internet brand leaders must therefore not become complacent. Traditional brands are already beginning to fight back with compelling and stress-free Web sites. BMW, Kodak, and Sony are good examples, in addition to those referred to in Chapter 6. Others such as Rizla, Pepsi, and Carling have created interactive Web sites, carefully designed to appeal to their target market segments. Virtual experiences such as these are complementing and, in some cases, boosting offline brand image, loyalty, and sales.

As the fight back by traditional brands continues, and offline giants gain online momentum, only a few of the cyberbrands that operate in the same markets are likely to succeed in the long term. As a consequence of this retaliation, the stock value of many Internet brands, currently so highly valued, may decline.

As the Internet marketplace becomes more cluttered and the

investment for branding increases, investors will want to know the real payback. They will look at profits and real values, rather than sales and hype. Brand valuation and appraisal techniques will provide the answers to many of the questions they ask. Companies will also increasingly turn to brand valuation to plan their optimum online and offline strategies for the Internet environment.

CASE STUDY
BRAND VALUATION
A global telecommunications company

U.K.-based consultants Brand Finance Plc (www.brandfinance.com) recently carried out a brand evaluation project for a global telecommunications company. The project focused on the company's home market and had the following objectives:

- To understand the role of the brand by customer and product segments, and against key competitors
- To develop a tracking and evaluation model to assist the drive toward a customer-oriented, brand-conscious culture
- To provide a financially robust value for the brand, for purposes of internal communications and for comparison with a brand valuation carried out two years ago

The financial valuation was of less significance than developing an understanding of how and where the brand was adding value to the company, and how this could be leveraged.

Given the rate of change within the telecommunications market, the issue of market segmentation was essential to developing brand strategies appropriate to the future. The evaluation was segmented by product categories within customer type. The brand evaluation model consisted of three work studies, namely:

1. Competitive analysis
To determine the competitive profile of the brand, and the risks attached to future earnings, Brand Finance Plc carried out a

competitive benchmarking study in each market segment. The client had a significant amount of competitive data that had not been systematically analyzed. Ten attributes were used to measure and track competitive performance. These were specifically determined for each product segment.

2. Consumer research

A trade-off research study was used to determine the Brand Value Added (BVA™), a measure of the brand's contribution to earnings. The trade-off data was analyzed to determine the weighting of the drivers of demand. In other words, the relative importance of brand, price, inertia, reach, and several service attributes was determined. The brand contribution and other driver weightings were compared across market segments and with key competitors. Service driver weightings were compared to consumer ideals.

3. Financial forecasts

The company's five-year forecasts were segmented by product category within customer segment. The three studies were integrated in a computerized model. While the output of each study yielded extremely useful information, it was the combination of outputs that had the most significant strategic implications. Market segments were simultaneously compared against the following criteria: forecast earnings growth, the brand's contribution to earnings, and its competitive position. Given the rapid change in the relative importance of product categories, this type of analysis provided actionable input to the following areas of marketing strategy:

- Brand architecture: The brand had been developed for a traditional telephony environment. The brand valuation enabled management to determine the extent of its contribution in the mobile, Internet, and solutions markets. Comparisons in the value added by the brand were made between market segments and with competing brands.

- *External communications*: The relative importance of the drivers of demand provided an input to marketing communications. Of specific interest in this regard was the difference between the brand's rating against specific service drivers and customers' stated importance of each driver.
- *Internal communications*: The brand valuation aids the central brand team to communicate the importance of the brand within the organization.
- *Performance tracking*: The brand evaluation model is currently being used to track brand performance.
- *Joint venture branding*: Knowledge gained from the valuation, supplemented by studies of other markets and brands, is being used to assess the value impact of branding decisions in international markets.

Brand valuation is going to be a fast-growth market. Emerging hi-tech brands have market capitalizations that defy logic, and huge sums have been paid for brand names. In the twenty-first century, when technology becomes more and more commonplace in business, and parity rules in all areas except brand image, it is the value of the brands that will help establish the true worth of companies.

THE FUTURE

The increasing amount of attention now being given to the valuation of brands adds more weight to the many compelling arguments in favor of building a strong brand.

We have seen over the last few years that world business markets have rapidly gone past the situation where establishing and keeping a prominent position was relatively easy, and parity relatively unknown. Nowadays, positioning is difficult and parity commonplace. Some people said that only strong companies will be able to survive in the new world. We would say that only strong brands will survive. And nowhere is this more true than in the hi-tech industries.

Whether you are running a bricks-and-mortar or a dot-com company, activities and transactions on the Web will take on an increasing amount of operations. To survive in the cold, impersonal world of technology, companies will have to get closer to the customer and give them warmer, less impersonal experiences. Web site journeys, for example, will need to become less cold and passive. Organizations with a heart and soul will be more appealing than those that fail to bring an emotional dimension to customer relationships.

As technological development progresses, and with more synergies taking place, the fragmented infrastructure that exists at present will over time mirror one another, while hi-tech products and services will become commodities. Creating differentiation in hi-tech industries through products and services is almost impossible due to extremely short product life cycles and rapid changes in technologies. It is too competitive. To stand out among all the clutter, to break parity, and occupy a favorable mind share, companies will have to rely more and more on the power of branding.

The true value of companies is already being reflected in the value attributed to the brand, so that those that provide the best consumer brand experience will be the ultimate winners. The branding of technology companies, products, and services is here to stay. The principles of branding remain, but the new world offers many challenges with regard to achieving the best customer brand experience.

Technology is like fashion in its tendency to change quickly. A dot-com company may well be old-fashioned in five to ten years' time; PCs could soon be things of the past. Companies wishing to continue to thrive in the business world need look no further than developing a powerful brand. With a strong brand identity and its resultant image, a company can achieve immortality, riding the waves of technological change.

Index

C

HI-TECH HI-TOUCH BRANDING

Creating Brand Power in the

Age of Technology